Financial Independence

IN THE 21ST CENTURY

Dwayne Burnell, MBA and
Suzanne Burnell, MSc

FinancialBallGame.com

Financial Independence in the 21st Century
©2012 Dwayne Burnell, MBA and Suzanne Burnell, MSc. All rights reserved.

ISBN: 978-0-9841335-4-3 (Paperback edition)
ISBN: 978-0-9841335-5-0 (ePub edition)
ISBN: 978-0-9841335-6-7 (Kindle/Mobi edition)
ISBN: 978-0-9841335-7-4 (ePDF edition)

Library of Congress Control Number: 2012939364
Personal Finance, Investments, Life Insurance

Financial Independence in the 21st Century
By Dwayne Burnell, MBA, and Suzanne Burnell, MSc

FinancialBallGamePublishing.com
PO Box 1089
Bothell, WA 98041
DwayneBurnell@FinancialBallGame.com
SuzanneBurnell@FinancialBallGame.com
www.FinancialBallGame.com
800-266-2971 (toll free)
425-286-7298

Printed in the United States of America

10 9 8 7 6 5 4 3 2 1

Book design by DesignForBooks.com
Cover photo by iStock©benedek

Suzanne and I dedicate this book to our parents

Frank and Christine Szojka
Denise Burnell

We also dedicate this book to those who provided additional guidance and support throughout our lives

Jolan Szojka
Bruce and Joan Gillis

Contents

CHAPTER **3** **A 21st CENTURY PARADIGM**

CHAPTER 6

MYTHS ABOUT WHOLE LIFE INSURANCE   97

Preface

It is tempting to follow the common financial planning advice repeated everywhere: "Stick with your 401(k). Ride out any stock market drops and hope for the best."

By adopting this conventional advice we put our money into financial vehicles that may *promise* great returns but cannot *guarantee* results. Our most common financial planning product, the mutual funds within a 401(k), do not produce predictable outcomes nor offer any performance guarantees. We're *hoping* to build a secure financial foundation on money that is at risk in the stock market.

It's important to realize that we have alternatives to chasing a rate of return. We don't have to live with the uncertain realities of the stock market or any investment market, for that matter, as our primary means of growing our money and our wealth.

In this book, we'd like you to put aside what you've learned about money or at least to entertain the possibility that some of what you have learned about money and financial planning may be incomplete, perhaps even faulty. It is our guiding belief that you deserve to live your life with the best possible lifetime financial strategy not the latest financial product.

By being open to new information and approaches, you can position yourself to have greater financial choices today and in the decades to come.

We live in challenging times. But we can choose how to face our future. Achieving financial independence and empowerment is a dynamic process and a journey. We invite you to join us.

Acknowledgements

Many people gave generously of their time, energy and wisdom to bring this book into being. Their contributions and insights are woven into the words and knowledge on every page.

We owe R. Nelson Nash sincere thanks for his book, *Becoming Your Own Banker*™ – *The Infinite Banking Concept*™, as reading it marked a true turning point in our financial understanding. We also appreciate Nelson Nash and David Stearns' gracious support.

Donald L. Blanton is a powerful force—providing insight and education as founder of the Circle of Wealth® System and The Private Reserve Strategy™. We have benefited greatly from Don's knowledge and passion regarding personal financial management.

The wisdom gained from conversations over the years with the following people helped shape the course and direction of this book. Our sincere gratitude to Terry O'Brien, and L. Ross Van Houten.

No effort as sustained as writing a book could be completed without the generous support of talented and skilled colleagues. Two such friends and professionals, Todd Avery and Frank Riedel IV, provided a thorough first review of the preliminary manuscript. Over years of friendship, Todd and Frank have also proven to be a wealth of knowledge, humor, and insight.

We have been fortunate to have many friends and colleagues generously make time to review manuscript drafts, offering keen perspectives which challenged us. Their invaluable comments and conversation helped us fashion this book into a more accessible and accurate work. Our sincere thanks to Jennifer Avery, John Baker, Maureen Baxter, Roger Bell, Sandy Brown, Kim Butler, Clay Campbell, Rick Darvis, Randall Davey, Chris Everett, Kevin Fink, Dave Francis, John Harding, Joe Kane, Lisa Klein, Todd Langford, Kevin Lasko, Brian and Karly Leyde, LeRoy Lopez, Diane and Greg Lozon, Shannon and Jim Madonna, BJ Mangrum, Michael McIntyre, Kathy Nielsen, Larry O'Brien, Sal Petruzzella, Rebecca and Bobby Rice, Angela Riedel, Mike Smela, Ron Them, Michael Thompson and Ann Todisco.

We feel grateful to have benefited from the patient and skillful assistance of three talented editors. Cassia Herman guided the project with a sense of vision, expertise and humor. Rachel Pearce Anderson brought a keen eye to copy editing and a thorough review of the book galleys. Our thanks also to our dear friend and editor, Margaret Shaw, for providing clarity on the overall tone and direction of the book.

Ted Therriault graciously proof-read the final manuscript. We are thankful for his skill and careful review.

Our special thanks to Shannon Madonna whose steadfast encouragement and generous administrative support is deeply appreciated.

We are grateful to Michael Rohani for the book cover design and for his talent and skill with the interior book layout.

Our sincere appreciation to the following Hurricane Financial January 2011 workshop participants for their supportive feedback on the first version of the case studies.

Kimm Alexander	John Harding	Bryan Sannes
Ewa Allen	Daniel Hoar	David Sannes
George Andrews	Robert Hughes Jr.	Lilliane Schmid
Al Banfe	Morgen Jackson	Rob Sheldon
Tommy Batts	Keith Jones	Scott Simpkins
Brian Bear	Edwin Kroger	Mike Smela
Bob Bergin	Jonathan LeBlanc	Tanya Solovieff
Lisa G. Bianco	Greg Lozon	Charles Taylor
Ken Billinger	Mike Marinzulich	Ginger Taylor
Keith Bohman	Anita McAllister	Joseph O. Thomas Jr.
Ken Brown	Jim Murphy	Michael Thompson
George Carbone	Robert Newhart Jr.	Curt VanDerzee
Lisa Cline	Dwight Nichols	Michael Wagner
John Clinger	Larry Nichols	Dru Watson
Gene Cross III	Loran O'Dell	Granville Waiters
Barbara Frye	Joe Orman	James Wright II
Gene Grass	Perry Russell	Don Yeoman
Rick Hainey	Matt Piver	Peni Yeoman
Don Harding	Terry Roberts	

1

Beginning the Journey

That fall day didn't start out to be particularly memorable. I stood in the kitchen with my wife, Suzanne. We'd just given our daughter a hug and sent her off to school. We watched her waltz away, her pink backpack swaying from side to side, and then Suzanne sat down at the kitchen table and started opening our daily mail.

"Good news," she said. "No bills, mostly junk mail today."

My eyes landed on the envelope containing our 401(k) statement. I opened it, glanced down the columns of numbers to the bottom dollar amount, and sighed.

"How is it that despite our continued portfolio balancing and rebalancing, our account isn't growing like all the gurus, articles, and books promise? At this rate, I'll be able to retire at 92. There's got to be a better way to manage our money than hoping we're going to catch a rise in the stock market."

Suzanne looked thoughtful.

"You know, you're right," she said. "We're capable and independent, we work hard. And we're smart enough to handle raising our child, managing our careers, and dealing with life challenges. So why are we willing to hand over total control of our money and our financial

… why are we willing to hand over total control of our money and our financial future to someone else?

future to someone else? And isn't investing in the stock market a risk to begin with? How do we know we won't lose it all? Then what? Isn't there a better way?"

It was a question we couldn't answer. But at that moment, we resolved to try. Our commitment to look for a better way to manage our family resources was the first humble step of an exciting journey. It began with examining how we were taught to handle our money and grew to challenging the common financial planning strategies we're all encouraged to embrace. Although the start was rather quiet, moving down this new path has dramatically changed the direction of our lives.

Our society has deeply conflicted attitudes toward making money and managing it. In one corner stands the ideology that wealth is everything. The more money you have the more successful you are considered. From this perspective, money seems to offer personal security, love, happiness, power, and freedom. Clearly, more is better.

Standing in the opposite corner is the philosophy that the accumulation of wealth is ill-conceived as a primary motivation for our lives, perhaps even evil. There is the notion that money corrupts or that accumulation of wealth is the concern of the spiritually inferior. Or the belief that spending money on items other than basic life necessities is a sign of greed and moral weakness.

Most of us harbor attitudes about money somewhere between these opposing ideologies. The singular pursuit of wealth above all else does seem ill-founded, yet we all need money to live. And who doesn't want a little extra financial buffer? What is wrong with planning for financial security for ourselves and those we love?

If we are not able to openly talk about some of the financial challenges we face, it is hard to address and resolve them.

One of the last taboos in our society is the open discussion of our personal financial situation: the values we hold about money, how much we make, and how and where we spend our money. This silence makes it hard for us to explore our attitudes and any limiting beliefs and knowledge we may have about money. If we are not able to openly talk about some of the financial challenges we face, it is hard to address and resolve them.

This is unfortunate. We need to be clear about our values around money, then educate ourselves in order to make the best decisions for our lives and our family.

Positioning Yourself for the 21st Century

In this book, Suzanne and I want to get you thinking about how to manage your money as you move forward in the 21st century. Consider how different the world was in the late 1970s when the 401(k) plan came into being. In the late 1970s, the Internet wasn't there. DVDs and cell phones had not been invented. Social networking, websites, and e-mail did not yet exist. People phoned each other using a dedicated landline that connected to the wall with a telephone wire. Many families had one-wage earner and one car. Most folks kept one job, or spent their lives in one profession or with one company. Many of our parents retired with pensions.

The reality of our lives is different now. Given the new world facing us in the 21st century, what we've done in the past isn't going to work in the future. And it may not be working in the present either.

We're not going to create financial strategies for ourselves that are flexible, responsive to change, and work in both a strong and weak economy, by doing what we've always done. The key to effective change is to seek new knowledge and be open to new ideas.

Common and routine financial advice is anchored in the past. Much financial planning advice is a strategy of looking in the rear-view mirror and talking about "past performance" of the stock market or the mutual fund within your 401(k) as a predictor of future growth. Does this really make sense when, like it or not, what we're facing as we look forward has not occurred before in history?

We truly face a new future. We need to accept the change that has arrived and not live in fear. Embracing change entails simple acknowledgement of our transformed conditions.

Common and routine financial advice is anchored in the past.

A Brave New World

As of January 2011, approximately 10,000 baby boomers *per day* (those born in the U.S. from 1946 to 1964) will become eligible to draw Social Security benefits. This volume of recipients for Social Security benefits is unprecedented and estimated to continue for another 20 years. To repeat, that's *10,000* new Social Security recipients per day for the next 20 years. So, applying a little math here, that's 10,000 new recipients times 365 days per year times 20 years: 73 million people applying for Social Security, not to mention other federal program benefits. Wow!

Figures reported by the Congressional Budget Office in an April 9, 2011 *Wall Street Journal* article on projected federal spending in fiscal year 2011 showed that the three big federal programs—Medicare, Medicaid, and Social Security—amounted to 42% of the entire federal budget projected for 2011.[1] By almost anyone's reckoning, looking to the 73 million people who will draw on these social programs in the next 20 years, these three programs are overcommitted and underfunded.

Our national debt is over 15 trillion dollars.[2] Since the estimated population of the U.S. is 310,506,107, each citizen's share of this debt is approximately $50,183 and climbing. Remember, **we** supply money to the government via taxes. Reducing this debt load will likely require increased taxes. Government programs and the services upon which we depend may be reduced or eliminated in budget cuts. We will then need to pay private providers and contractors directly to replace these services.

The stock market has always been volatile. However, we live in an Internet and social media age that allows almost instantaneous

---

1. Carol E. Lee, "Deadline Drama for Budget: Impasse Tested the Clock," *Wall Street Journal*, April 9-10, 2011.

2. As of March 10, 2012, the national debt was $15,582,079,000,000. Source: Monthly Statement of the Public Debt (MSPD) and Downloadable Files, Treasury Direct, accessed March 31, 2012, http://www.treasurydirect.gov/govt/reports/pd/mspd/mspd.htm.

communication of world events. The markets react exceedingly quickly to political events and economic circumstances. As we are all too well aware, what happens around the world, whether it is in Japan, China, Greece, or the Middle East, directly affects our economy and our lives. We also face new environmental and ecological challenges. We live in an age of accelerating change through communications.

Despite all these conditions never before experienced in the history of the world, we continue to be taught the standard financial line, which is based upon looking back at trends and averages from the Depression era and World War II. Many people know that past trends are not a truly accurate predictor of future performance, and yet we are still advised to just stay in the stock market. Really? Is this the best financial strategy for our lifetime? Is this the only option we have?

Who's on First?

Baseball is considered America's pastime. Let's think for a moment about Major League Baseball players. Many kids grow up with a dream to play Major League Baseball for a living. How do those that want to play professional ball get to the Majors? Do they spend their time trying to find the right bat, the right ball, the ultimate glove, or a uniform with trendy colors? Or do they place their effort in practicing baseball skills, learning game rules, focusing on strategy, and increasing their knowledge of their sport? Which approach do you think will yield the best result?

To make it as a Major League Baseball professional, the baseball player invests in knowledge and practice to succeed. He doesn't hope that the right product (be it ball, bat, uniform, or glove) will make the difference for him.

When it comes to finances and lifelong financial strategy, most of us have been chasing a product. We hope to find the right investment product that will give us a high rate of return. We are like the kid that

. . . past trends are not a truly accurate predictor of future performance, and yet we are still advised to just stay in the stock market.

When it comes to finances and lifelong financial strategy, most of us have been chasing a product.

wants to make it to the Majors and thinks the right product—bat or glove—will take him there.

Preparing to Move Forward with Confidence

. . . it is possible to achieve financial independence with a relatively modest income.

Many people spend a lifetime worrying about their money. They worry about meeting their daily expenses, being able to save for their children's education, and for their own retirement. People also fear losing their money if they become unemployed or through the loss of capital in their investments. It doesn't have to be this way. There is an alternative approach that can remove the weight of anxiety and fear.

Contrary to much of the financial rhetoric, it *is* possible to achieve financial independence with a relatively modest income. You don't have to be Bill Gates or Warren Buffett to reach a place where you are free of worry about whether your money will be available to you when you need it, or when you are ready to retire.

Instead of focusing on finding the "right" financial product, it will benefit us much more to look at our lifetime goals and increase our financial knowledge and skill. In being open to new information and approaches, we can position ourselves to have greater financial choices today and in the decades to come.

Consider that the goal is to build a financial strategy that will truly last a lifetime. Once we develop our skill and our financial knowledge, then we are in a position to thoughtfully *choose* the appropriate financial products that fit into and support this strategy.

Unfortunately, many of us have placed money in the stock market, via our 401(k) investments, that we cannot afford to lose.

Entering the stock market, real estate, or other investment opportunities to strategically enhance your wealth, using money *you **can** afford to lose,* is a very different strategy than placing retirement money *you **cannot** afford to lose* in an unpredictable stock or real estate market. Unfortunately, many of us have placed money in the stock market, via our 401(k) investments, that we cannot afford to lose.

We are not saying "never invest." Placing money that is **not** critical to your financial survival in an investment with a potential for a higher rate of return can be an important component of a financial strategy. Investments can and do yield high returns. Sometimes. However, too much focus on a rate of return blinds us to other elements that are important in managing money and growing wealth.

So why not step back and think about your money in a different way? It is truly possible to develop a stable and predictable financial strategy that will work with your needs and wants, and congruently serve your long-term goals.

To be clear, Suzanne and I don't believe in "get rich quick" schemes or advice that suggests that with this or that deal, you'll be set for life. It's true that some people will get rich on a single deal. It's also true that many of us will lose a lot of our savings chasing that one magic opportunity. But our financial lives don't have to be lived on the edge, sweat beading on our foreheads as we open our latest investment statement. This is hardly the type of excitement Suzanne and I crave.

What we *do* believe is that with a little knowledge you can set yourself on a different financial path. One that enables you and your family to reach a level of financial security, control, and independence you might never have thought possible. To get to this point, though, requires a willingness to explore the new and the different.

This book seeks to stretch your knowledge and your comfort zone by challenging the commonly-held beliefs and attitudes most of us have learned and adopted about money. It is our guiding belief that you deserve to live your life with the best possible lifetime financial strategy built upon a cornerstone of solid knowledge.

. . . with a little knowledge you can set yourself on a different financial path.

A Financial Paradigm Shift

Let's talk for a moment about change and growth. Each of us has many ways of looking at the world.

An event happens. Perhaps someone laughs while looking at us. The only real "fact" we have is that they laughed. But we look at this event through the filter of our own experience and values. We tell ourselves a story about what just happened—they like us, they are happy or they are laughing at us. Or, if we don't know them, we may not register a reaction.

How we react depends upon our story about the event. We interpret everything we experience through the lens of how we view the world. Rarely does it occur to us to question the accuracy or completeness of our view.

When we deeply consider new information this can shift our thinking. This is what the term "paradigm shift" means—a change from one way of thinking to another.

A paradigm shift is essentially a perceptual transformation. It's a different way of seeing that allows us to forge new solutions to complex problems. A shift in perspective allows people to look at vexing problems in a new way, develop more effective solutions, and be open to new knowledge.

Stephen Covey discussed social paradigm shifts in his bestseller, *The 7 Habits of Highly Effective People.* Covey wrote that *"the more we are aware of our basic paradigms, maps, or assumptions, and the extent to which we have been influenced by our experience, the more we can take responsibility for those paradigms, examine them, test them against reality, listen to others and be open to their perceptions, thereby getting a larger picture and a far more objective view."*[3]

Paradigm shifts are not new. Throughout collective history our paradigms have shifted. The way we view the world has necessarily changed to make way for greater knowledge and more in-depth

> The voyage of discovery is not in seeking new landscapes but in having new eyes.
>
> —MARCEL PROUST

3. Stephen R. Covey, *The 7 Habits of Highly Effective People, Powerful Lessons in Personal Change* (New York, NY: Simon & Schuster Inc., 1989), page 29.

understanding. Witness the growth from our belief that the sun revolves around the earth to our understanding of the earth as part of a solar system that revolves around the sun. When Christopher Columbus set sail the commonly held view was that the world was flat. Now we know more.

Shifting our personal paradigm means that we expand our understanding of how we interpret events, people, our environment, and possibly all of life itself. Changing how we see a particular situation can have a dramatic effect on the choices we make now and in the future.

What we perceive depends on the perspective we take. This is especially true when it comes to our own money and financial paradigm. We view our situation through a lens or with knowledge that may be outdated or incomplete. It takes courage to be open to change. But once we shift our point of view, a doorway may open to new solutions for our current dilemma.

> "The significant problems we face cannot be solved at the same level of thinking we were at when we created them."
>
> —ALBERT EINSTEIN

A shift in your financial paradigm takes time, effort, and thought. Suzanne and I are asking for a little of these elements, plus a willingness to process new information. We'd like you to take this journey with us, to explore a different approach.

No matter where we want to go, we must begin our journey where we are. So let's start the journey together by examining our current beliefs with respect to money: the late 20th century financial paradigm.

2

The Late 20th Century Financial Paradigm

It's hard to believe that the fundamental way we plan for retirement in the U.S. today really only emerged 34 years ago. That's right—the qualified plan (for many of us this is a 401(k))—was legislated into reality in 1978.

Qualified Plans

So What is a Qualified Plan?

A *qualified plan* is an investment vehicle that qualifies for special tax treatment under the Internal Revenue Code.

Qualified plans include the 401(k) and 403(b) plans, the traditional Individual Retirement Account (IRA), the Keogh Plan, Simplified Employee Pension Individual Retirement Account (SEP-IRA), Roth IRA, Savings Incentive Match Plan for Employees (SIMPLE), and the Stretch IRA.

There are also other qualified plans that are not related to retirement. An example of one such plan is the Health Savings Account (HSA).

The Origin of the 401(k)

The 401(k) plan was the original qualified plan. This plan was named for a section of the Internal Revenue Code: Section 401(k). It was a congressional action intended to offer taxpayers tax breaks on deferred income. At that time, the 401(k) plan was seen as a way for people to put aside money for retirement *outside* of, and *in addition* to, the traditional pension retirement plan. Since 401(k) contributions were designed to be pre-tax, the money would be placed into some sort of investment product (usually a mutual fund) and taxed in the future at the time the money would be withdrawn.

While the 401(k) was never intended to replace retirement pension plans, this is largely what has happened over the past 34 years. During the early years of the 401(k), more than 170,000 traditional pension plans existed in the U.S. As of 2008, there were less than 47,000 pension plans still in existence.[1] Many companies found it more economical to offer 401(k) plans with a matching contribution than to manage pension funds.

The Decline and Fall of Pension Plans

The 401(k) was designed to be the icing on the retirement planning cake. But, in a twist of fate, since its inception it has become the whole cake. More than 65 million 401(k) accounts now allow participants to invest in stocks, bonds, and mutual funds, some with matching funds from employers. These accounts helped spark a financial-industry boom, funneling billions into mutual funds and the stock market.[2]

---

1. Daniel R. Solin, *The Smartest 401(k)* Book You'll Ever Read, Maximize Your Retirement Savings . . . the Smart Way! (*Smartest 403(b) and 457(b), too!)* (New York, NY: Penguin Group (USA) Inc., 2008).

2. Alyssa Fetini, "A Brief History of: The 401(k)," *Time Magazine*, October 16, 2008, accessed April 29, 2011, http://www.time.com/time/magazine/article/0,9171,1851124,00.html.

With the advent of the 401(k) plan, we have seen a fundamental shift in our thinking about investment in the stock market. Prior to 1978, investing in the stock market was primarily the arena of the wealthy. It was seen as a risky way to make money. Average Americans saved money in their bank accounts, paid off their mortgage or purchased real estate or bonds, and generally considered their company pension to be the core of their retirement planning. Investing in the stock market was acknowledged as offering the possibility to garner significant returns. But everyone also seemed to understand clearly that the possibility of heady returns was accompanied by the potential of loss of the original investment.

> "It can be very easy to drift off into a sea of misinformation and drown in the sole pursuit of a magic product."
>
> —DONALD L. BLANTON

401(k) Performance

It's intriguing to stand back and think about the overall performance of the typical 401(k) plan with mutual funds invested in the stock market. Here we are, 34 years after the inception of the 401(k) plan, and we still hear the often-quoted average 8 to 10% stock market growth rate per year. Theoretically, most of us should be feeling pretty good about our 401(k) or other qualified plan performance right now.

Yet, according to a May 11, 2011 report by the Fidelity Investment Company Institute, Americans' 401(k) savings in the first quarter of 2011 reached a record balance of $74,900.[3] That's right, the average American has only $74,900 invested for retirement. This news was greeted with delight and as evidence of stock market resurgence. But let's remember that this number reflects *average* savings, so many 401(k) balances are significantly lower than this figure.

---

3. Dawn Kawamoto. "Average 401(k) Balances Hit a Record High in First Quarter," *Daily Finance*, accessed May 25, 2011, http://www.dailyfinance.com/2011/05/12/401k-balances-record-high-first-quarter.

More to the point, the average of $74,900 in 401(k) plans reflects an all-time high. Really? Wow. Shouldn't we all be doing better by now if we were getting a steady 8% growth in our qualified plan funds over the last 34 years? Who can afford to retire and live out their days on $74,900?

The Bottom Line

What has really happened since the inception of the 401(k) and other qualified plans is that investment risk shifted from the employer and has become completely the employee's burden. The employee has exchanged the promise of a company benefit upon retirement for the ability to control his or her investment.

In contrast to a pension fund, your 401(k) plan or other qualified plan actually promises *nothing* with respect to a retirement benefit from the company.

... your 401(k) plan or other qualified plan actually promises nothing with respect to a retirement benefit from the company.

Do You Know Where Your Money Is?

Let's take a closer look at this issue of investing within your 401(k) or other qualified plan. Saving and investing are two very distinct concepts. Your savings consist of money that you don't want to lose. Money you invest is money that is subject to the risk of loss.

Think about mutual funds. Stock mutual funds are typically an investment product designed for growth. As such, they carry a higher risk of loss of our principal than a savings vehicle such as a certificate of deposit (CD). We *save* in our CD or Money Market accounts; we *invest* our money in financial vehicles like mutual funds or real estate.

Yet, in the marketplace, we often hear and read about "*saving* for retirement with mutual funds within our 401(k)." This is not accurate. A lot of retirement "savings" accounts are really retirement "investment" accounts. By confusing and blending the fundamental concepts of saving and investing, we confuse the risk associated with our money. By not being clear about whether our money is in a savings or an investment product, we can end up believing that our money is less exposed to risk, and thereby safer, than it really is.

A Closer Look at the Late 20th Century Paradigm

Throughout the last 30 or so years we have been exhorted and encouraged to place a great deal of reliance on qualified plans, such as our 401(k), to fund our retirement. Qualified plans are supposed to provide us with the income we need in retirement. It's the approach that is embodied by the financial counsel we hear or read every day:

"Stay in the stock market, ride out the down-turn, the market will rebound."

"Invest for the long-term."

"Focus on your rate of return."

Let's consider the 401(k) plan once more. Many people have a very large percentage (if not all) of their retirement money situated within mutual funds in a 401(k). To restate: a mutual fund is an *investment* vehicle, subject to loss at any time.

When you contribute money to a mutual fund, you join hundreds or thousands of other investors whose money is pooled together to invest in stocks, bonds, money market instruments, or other similar assets. While the U.S. government allows you to contribute to your qualified plan before-tax, you pay a 10% withdrawal penalty (plus any additional income tax the following April) for the privilege of removing the money from this program if you withdraw it before you reach age 59½. And you pay income tax on both your money and its growth after age 59½.

Ironically, you are also penalized if you want to keep your money within your 401(k) or other qualified plan. In fact, by age 70½, you

By not being clear about whether our money is in a savings or an investment product, we can end up believing that our money is less exposed to risk, and thereby safer, than it really is.

are forced to take "Required Minimum Distributions." Required Minimum Distributions (RMDs) refer to the minimum amount of money that a qualified plan owner must withdraw annually starting with the year that he or she reaches 70½ years of age. There is a 50% penalty on the amount below the RMD that you leave inside your qualified plan. Why regulate the distributions from qualified plans? Because the government wants to collect income tax on the money which the qualified plan participant has deferred paying for many years.

You do not have control over how your mutual funds will perform in the marketplace.

Lack of Control, Rate of Return, and Capital Loss

You *do not* have control over how your mutual funds will perform in the marketplace. Clearly, we all want the stock market to go up and the value of our 401(k) funds to increase. But what if this doesn't happen and you lose money inside your qualified plan?

Mutual funds are operated by money managers. Does the fund manager lose money when you lose money? The money manager may lose sleep, but not money. The fund manager still gets paid and the institutions still collect their fees. You're the only one who loses. *Your money is at risk, not theirs.* Their ultimate loss is that they may lose you as a client. However, it's *you* who have to endure the consequences of losing your hard-earned money.

When you are chasing a rate of return, you are *not* focused on what would happen if you lost your principal. Instead you concentrate your energy on possible gains. You do not think about how you would cope if you lost some or all of your initial investment.

Loss of your original capital is critically important to consider since the greater your loss, the harder it is just to get back to your starting point. When you combine the loss of your original capital with the erosion of your wealth due to taxes, inflation, and fees, the financial result can be, and often is, devastating. Also, as you get older, you have less time to recover from the effect of loss.

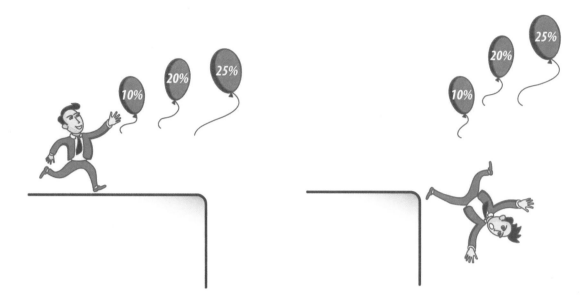

Chasing a Rate of Return

Let's take a closer look at the core components of our late 20th century financial thinking. In this case, what you don't know ***can*** hurt you.

Understanding "Rate of Return"

The intense focus on chasing a "rate of return" or "return on investment" comes at a high cost. By allowing rate of return to become the primary consideration when we look at financial vehicles, we inadvertently eliminate many financial options available to us. Not to mention that the concept of rate of return can be confusing if not down-right misleading.

Consider the concept of an "average" rate of return. This is how many investment companies and mutual funds report their results. We will use a simplified analysis of how the average rate of return is calculated over an arbitrary time period, say four years.

Table 1 shows the market fluctuation over a four-year period. Our example demonstrates that the first year rate of return on your invested money is 100%. The next year, the market drops and your investment value decreases by 50%. The year after that, the market goes up 100%, then down once more. At the end of year four, you have achieved an "average annual rate of return" of 25%. At this point, opening up your statement and seeing that you have received an average annual rate of return on your investment of 25%, you might be tempted to pull out the champagne.

But wait.

Before you uncork that celebratory bottle, let's take another look at exactly the same scenario. This time, instead of using percentages, let's follow your money. In Table 2, in addition to the percentage rate of return, take a close look at how your money actually performed over this four-year period. We'll assume you start with a balance of $10,000 in your investment.

Table 1: Average Rate of Return

Year	Market
1	+100%
2	−50%
3	+100%
4	−50%
Average Rate of Return	+25%

Table 2: Following Your Money Through an Average Rate of Return of 25%

Year	Market	Starting Balance	Ending Balance
1	+100%	$10,000	$20,000
2	−50%	$20,000	$10,000
3	+100%	$10,000	$20,000
4	−50%	$20,000	$10,000
Average Rate of Return = +25%			

Notice that although you've achieved an average rate of return of 25%, at the end of year four, your money has not grown. Why? Well, because when we think of a 25% average annual rate of return over four years, most people think of a *linear progression* of 25% compounded each and every year.

What this means is that, **contrary to reality,** we calculate our rate of return as linear compounded growth, as follows:

Year 1: $10,000 x 1.25 = $12,500
Year 2: $12,500 x 1.25 = $15,625
Year 3: $15,625 x 1.25 = $19,531
Year 4: $19,531 x 1.25 = $24,414

This is **not** correct if your money is in the market.

Average rate of return is not the same as compound interest. In reality, the path your investment money follows is shown in Table 2. What this means is that even though you received an average rate of return of 25% on your money over four years, your investment is **not** 25% larger, year by year, over the four-year period.

The disappointing truth is that at the end of this four-year period, you will most likely have less capital than you started with because along the way there have been sales charges, fees, and other expenses (which we have not accounted for in the above example).

If this example is a surprise to you, you are not alone. Many of us are caught off-guard and surprised by the reality of the math behind the money.

Average rate of return is not the same as compound interest.

Understanding the Impact of Investment Capital Loss

Our investments ride the ups and downs of the stock market. But we are often unaware of how this fluctuation impacts their long-term growth. It's worth taking a closer look at the effect of losing part of your original principal. What most of us don't realize is that *once you've lost a portion of your starting capital, it takes more time and a higher rate of return for your remaining capital to just get back to its original value.* And you have to earn the money all over again to be able to reinvest it.

To clarify this concept, we've created a series of snapshots (Tables 3 through 6) that compare what would happen to your money if you placed it in a savings vehicle (where your money receives interest at a rate of 5% per year) with how your money will grow in an investment vehicle receiving a rate of return of 8% (as is often promised in the stock market).

Table 3 shows the difference in the growth of your money when your investment does not suffer any losses. This scenario is not representative of stock market behavior. It is, though, how we are often encouraged to think about investing. The potential for loss is minimized, while the possible rate of return is highlighted.

Look at Table 3. Without any loss, your investment makes 8% in the stock market and easily outperforms the savings vehicle. Starting with $10,000 in each account, after Year 1, your investment account is $300 ahead (Line **1**, Table 3).

By Year 5, the difference in growth between your investment account and the savings vehicle is $1,930 (Line **2**, Table 3).

At Year 10, the investment account has outperformed the savings vehicle by $5,300 (Line **3**, Table 3). Wow! This growth is what we all want. It's the story we hear when we talk to anyone trying to encourage us to invest in their accounts or with their product or company. For goodness sake, why would we waste time placing our money in a savings vehicle when this type of growth is available to us in the investment world?

Why? Because what is not factored into this example in Table 3 is the impact of a ***single*** event of capital loss. What happens if you have just one year in which the money inside your mutual fund or real estate investment loses 20%? In other words, your investment receives an 8% rate of return for nine years and then for just one year experiences a 20% drop instead of 8% growth.

Let's look at the impact of taking this one-time loss at different times over that 10-year period: Year 1, Year 5, and Year 10. The results of this analysis are summarized in Tables 4, 5, and 6.[4]

4. The Circle of Wealth® System. Money *Trax*, Inc., COW Software: *Toolbox/Calculators/ Compound versus Speculation Calculator,* Version 2012.0, Cow College Pre-Release, January 2012 (Tables 3 through 6 were generated using this software).

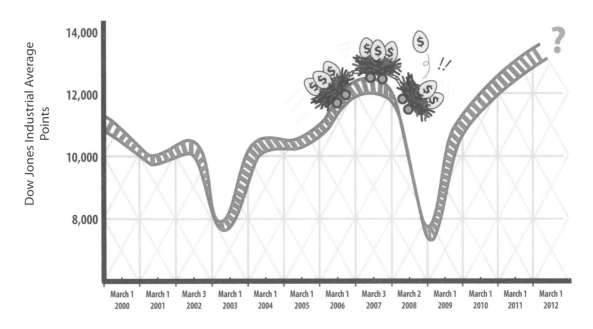

Riding the Stock Market Roller Coaster with Your Retirement

As Tables 4 through 6 demonstrate, when we look at the impact of taking a 20% loss in rate of return for *one* year but otherwise receiving a steady rate of return of 8% per year on our investment for nine years, two striking results emerge at the end of the 10-year period:

1. The savings vehicle with 5% interest yields slightly more money ($297) than the 8% investment vehicle.

2. The timing of the one-time 20% loss (i.e., whether it occurred at the beginning, middle, or the end of the investment period) does *not* impact the final balance. In other words, ***the effect of just one period of capital loss at any point over the investment period exerts a long-lasting impact on your wealth.***

Table 3 — Comparison of 5% Compound Interest versus 8% Rate of Return

Year	Savings Vehicle End of Year Balance (Starting Principal of $10,000) Interest Rate 5%		Investment Account End of Year Balance (Starting Principal of $10,000) Rate of Return 8%		Difference Investment Account Value minus Savings Vehicle Value
① 1[1]	5%	$10,500	8%	$10,800	$300
2	5%	$11,025	8%	$11,664	$639
3	5%	$11,576	8%	$12,597	$1,021
4	5%	$12,155	8%	$13,605	$1,450
② 5	5%	$12,763	8%	$14,693	$1,930
6	5%	$13,401	8%	$15,869	$2,468
7	5%	$14,071	8%	$17,138	$3,067
8	5%	$14,755	8%	$18,509	$3,754
9	5%	$15,513	8%	$19,990	$4,477
③ 10	5%	$16,289	8%	$21,589	$5,300

Notes

1. Initial contribution (at beginning of Year 1) is $10,000

Assumptions

1. Annual savings vehicle interest rate is 5%
2. Rate of return (speculation) is set at 8%
3. No account fees, service charges, commissions, or taxes were included in this example

Table 4 — Comparison of 5% Interest with 8% Rate of Return
One Capital Loss Event (20%) for Investment Account—Year 1

Year	Savings Vehicle End of Year Balance (Starting Principal of $10,000) Interest Rate 5%		Investment Account End of Year Balance (Starting Principal of $10,000) Interest Rate 8%		Difference Investment Account Value minus Savings Vehicle Value
1	5%	$10,500	(20%)[1]	$8,000	$ (2,500)[2]
2	5%	$11,025	8%	$8,640	$ (2,385)
3	5%	$11,576	8%	$9,331	$ (2,245)
4	5%	$12,155	8%	$10,078	$ (2,077)
5	5%	$12,763	8%	$10,884	$ (1,879)
6	5%	$13,401	8%	$11,755	$ (1,646)
7	5%	$14,071	8%	$12,695	$ (1,376)
8	5%	$14,755	8%	$13,711	$ (1,044)
9	5%	$15,513	8%	$14,807	$ (706)
10	5%	$16,289	8%	$15,992	$ (297)

Notes

1. Highlighted row indicates year of 20% loss in investment rate of return (i.e., $10,000 x 20% = $2,000; $10,000 minus $2,000 = $8,000)
2. Difference in Year 1 account values: $8,000 minus $10,500 = $ (2,500)

Assumptions

1. Initial contribution (at beginning of Year 1) is $10,000
2. Annual savings vehicle interest rate is 5%
3. Rate of return (speculation) is set at 8%
4. No account fees, service charges, commissions, or taxes were included in this example

Table **5**	Comparison of 5% Interest with 8% Rate of Return One Capital Loss Event (20%) for Investment Account—Year 5		
Year	Savings Vehicle End of Year Balance *(Starting Principal of $10,000)* **Interest Rate 5%**	Investment Account End of Year Balance *(Starting Principal of $10,000)* **Rate of Return 8%**	Difference **Investment Account Value minus Savings Vehicle Value**
1	5% $10,500	8% $10,800	$300
2	5% $11,025	8% $11,664	$639
3	5% $11,576	8% $12,597	$1,021
4	5% $12,155	8% $13,605	$1,450
5	5% $12,763	(20%)[1] $10,884	$ (1,879)[2]
6	5% $13,401	8% $11,755	$ (1,646)
7	5% $14,071	8% $12,695	$ (1,376)
8	5% $14,755	8% $13,711	$ (1,044)
9	5% $15,513	8% $14,807	$ (706)
10	5% $16,289	8% $15,992	$ (297)

Notes

1. Highlighted row indicates year of 20% loss in investment rate of return (i.e., $13,605 x 20% = $2,721; $13,605 minus $2,721 = $10,884)
2. Difference in Year 5 account values: $10,884 minus $12,763 = $ (1,879)

Assumptions

1. Initial contribution (at beginning of Year 1) is $10,000
2. Annual savings vehicle interest rate is 5%
3. Rate of return (speculation) is set at 8%
4. No account fees, service charges, commissions, or taxes were included in this example

Comparison of 5% Interest with 8% Rate of Return
One Capital Loss Event (20%) for Investment Account—Year 10

Year	Savings Vehicle End of Year Balance (Starting Principal of $10,000) Interest Rate 5%		Investment Account End of Year Balance (Starting Principal of $10,000) Rate of Return 8%		Difference Investment Account Value minus Savings Vehicle Value
1	5%	$10,500	8%	$10,800	$300
2	5%	$11,025	8%	$11,664	$639
3	5%	$11,576	8%	$12,597	$1,021
4	5%	$12,155	8%	$13,605	$1,450
5	5%	$12,763	8%	$14,693	$1,930
6	5%	$13,401	8%	$15,869	$2,468
7	5%	$14,071	8%	$17,138	$3,067
8	5%	$14,755	8%	$18,509	$3,754
9	5%	$15,513	8%	$19,990	$4,477
10	5%	$16,289	(20%)[1]	$15,992	$ (297)[2]

Notes

1. Highlighted row indicates year of 20% loss in investment rate of return (i.e., $19,990 x 20% = $3,998; $19,990 minus $3,998 = $15,992)
2. Difference in Year 10 account values: $15,992 minus $16,289 = $ (297)

Assumptions

1. Initial contribution (at beginning of Year 1) is $10,000
2. Annual savings vehicle interest rate is 5%
3. Rate of return (speculation) is set at 8%
4. No account fees, service charges, commissions, or taxes were included in this example

This sample scenario is dramatic. So is the effect of capital loss on your financial well-being. This example illustrates just how hard it is to grow your money within an investment vehicle in which your principal is subject to loss.

The Flow of Your Money

It might seem odd to associate a static object like a quarter or a dollar bill with movement. But we use such terms as "cash flow" and "revenue stream" to describe how money enters our world, how we use it, and where it goes. Even the word "income" effectively means an entrance or influx.[5]

... the key to financial control and independence is in how you manage the flow of your money.

Your Financial Life Cycle

Any number of metaphors can describe how money comes into your world and leaves it. More important than the metaphor is the reality that the key to financial control and independence is in how you manage the flow of your money. Money entering your personal financial world could come from your job, social security, your pension, savings, an inheritance, investments, or other sources (trusts, annuities, etc). Most people want to grow their wealth, and they focus on the "incoming" or inflow side of the financial life cycle as they look at the rate of return on their investments.

... most of us pay little attention to the ways our hard-earned money flows away from us.

What people often neglect is the other side of this cycle: *the out-flow* of money. It is such a simple and unglamorous point. But after all that effort to make money and search out investment products that promise a great rate of return, most of us pay little attention to the ways our hard-earned money flows away from us.

5. *Merriam-Webster's Collegiate Dictionary,* 11th Edition (Springfield, Massachusetts, Merriam-Webster Inc., 2005).

If you're like most people, you are often keenly aware of the cost of life needs and choices. But these expenses are not what we're talking about here. We are referring to the less obvious leaks in our financial system—the ways that money quietly flows out of our financial world with little or no thought, or even direct action on our part.

As our discussion on saving versus the impact of capital loss shows, just plugging the leaks in your financial system can result in a major positive growth to your long-term wealth.

You cannot control the erosive impact of inflation on your purchasing power. However, you do have far more control than you realize over many of the leaks in your financial system.

Let's examine four direct ways and one indirect way that money needlessly seeps out of your financial system.

. . . you do have far more control than you realize over many of the leaks in your financial system.

Direct Outflow

Taxes

Taxes of all shapes and size are a reality of life. We have taxes on our income, capital gains, property, purchases (sales tax), and on our cell phone, cable, and internet services, to name a few.

Paying some of these taxes may be inevitable and even necessary. In the case of income tax, we want to meet our civic responsibility and pay our fair share but not more. How we structure and time the income coming into our life will determine how much income tax we pay now and in retirement.

Take investment income, for example. If we neglect to consider the amount of money we pay in taxes on that income, we are making a financial mistake. With a little strategic planning, we may reduce our tax burden and subsequently the money that flows away from us by paying too much in taxes.

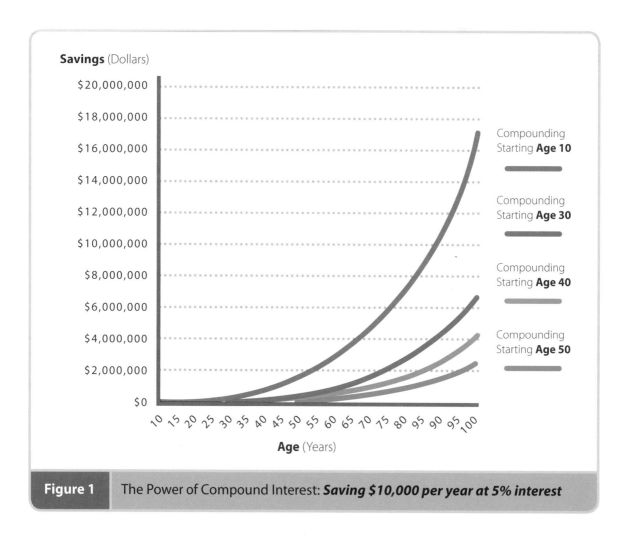

Savings (Dollars)

Figure 1 | The Power of Compound Interest: *Saving $10,000 per year at 5% interest*

Capital loss

As we illustrated in Tables 4 through 6, the effect of *just one* period of capital loss has a long-lasting negative impact on your wealth. Of course, one option is to bury your money in a coffee tin in the back yard. Given the losses some of our investments have sustained over the past few years, this approach might be starting to look pretty good.

But when your money is buried or inaccessible, it cannot work for you or grow at all. If we can prevent the loss of our original principal (or capital) in the first place, then we are not continually coming from behind to try and catch up. *We start on a firmer financial footing when we are growing money not subject to loss.*

Remember the power of compound interest. Compound interest is paid on the original principal and on the accumulated interest.

Figure 1 illustrates the simple, effective power of compound interest. The graph illustrates the savings potential starting at different ages (10, 30, 40, and 50) and saving $10,000 per year with 5% interest on this money. Even starting a savings program such as this one at age 40, the power of compound interest means you could save almost half a million dollars ($536,691) by age 65 and just over 1 million dollars by age 70.

It's not glamorous. It's not exciting. But it is steady, predictable, and sustainable growth over your lifetime. It's also the power of not having to recover from the erosion, or loss, of your principal.

Remember the power of compound interest.

Payment of loan interest to others

When you ask for a loan and borrow money, whether it is from a financial institution or a credit card, you are not in control of the interest rate and repayment terms. The bank makes a loan offer and you either accept their terms and conditions or not. If you don't accept their terms, you don't get the loan.

Many of us pay loan interest on our cars, homes, and other purchases. We pay high interest rates on many of our credit cards. Credit card interest can be particularly tricky. Miss one payment and the interest rate on your balance can change from your current rate to one as high as 29.99%. It can take years to pay off credit card debt when you are paying 29.99% interest.

Payment of interest can be a significant drain on your household income. Often, we feel trapped because we need access to credit, but the cost of this credit can be debilitating. A key way to manage your household economy is to remove the burden of high interest rate payments and the structured schedule under which you repay your loan.

A key way to manage your household economy is to remove the burden of high interest rate payments . . .

Fees and miscellaneous service charges to others

Many of us pay a large amount of money to others to manage our money. We pay ATM fees, debit card fees, account maintenance, and other transaction fees to financial institutions; we pay transfer fees, paper fees, service charges, and commissions on our mutual funds.

If we reduce the fees, service charges, and interest we pay to others, we don't need to earn as much on our money because we are not losing so much. In fact, Don Blanton (Money*Trax*, Inc.) sums it up when he says, *"There is more opportunity in preventing losses than in chasing gains."* [6]

Frank and Ernest

Indirect Outflow

Lost opportunity cost

The money that flows away from us due to taxes, capital loss, and loan interest, fees, and service charges, does not come back to us. As a consequence, we lose the opportunity to save this money and use it for the rest of our lives. We also lose the chance to have this money work for us, whether it is in a savings or investment vehicle.

---

6. Don Blanton, 2011. Money*Trax*, Inc., The *Circle of Wealth® System.*

You may also hear the conventional "wisdom" that you can afford to take more investment and money risks when you are young. The rationale goes that if you risk and lose money, it is okay because you have time to recover. However, losing dollars at a young age means *you lose the earning power of this money for the rest of your life.*

Why should you take a loss at any age?

Let's illustrate this lost opportunity cost with an example. Suppose at age 20 you lose $1,000 in an investment. If you had simply placed this money in a savings vehicle and received 5% interest on this until age 65 you would have accumulated $8,985.

Consider that in many instances your losses are not limited to $1,000. Suppose instead of $1,000 you lost a total of $5,000 ($1,000 each year) in your mutual fund from age 20 through 24. If you had placed this $1,000 each year in a savings vehicle over five years at 5% interest, instead of the market, at age 65 you would have had $40,846.

Why should you take a loss at any age?

Managing Your Money

You must earn and spend money to live, to grow, and to care for yourselves and your family. However, your lifetime earnings are eroded when your money flows away from you through taxes, capital loss, and via the payment of loan interest, fees, and service charges. When you let money flow out of your financial system, you also compound your loss by not being able to use this money for the rest of your life. By simply being aware of the significant negative impact of this outflow, you can start to consider how to minimize or eliminate these losses.

You can't control the global economy. You can't control the national or regional economy. You don't even have control over your local economy. The only situation over which you have control is your household economy.

The only situation over which you have control is your household economy.

You can manage your household economy by controlling how your money moves—both incoming and outgoing. By aggressively managing your tax liability, minimizing the impact of capital loss, and reducing fees and loan interest you pay to others, you take an important step forward toward financial independence and the successful growth of your own wealth.

Putting it All Together: Average Rate of Return, Capital Loss, and the Impact of Fees

As we round the corner and conclude Chapter 2, you now possess a stronger understanding of how rate of return and investment capital loss impact your money and its growth.

Now we're going to put it all together. We will look at two examples to demonstrate how a fluctuating rate of return, capital loss, *and* standard sales commission and mutual fund fees can affect your investment growth.

In each example, we provide a baseline situation without the impact of a sales commission and mutual fund fees. The second part of the example illustrates the impact of adding a single, one-time standard sales commission of 5% along with an annual mutual fund fee of 2%. While the percentages used for sales commissions and mutual fund fees vary among products and companies, these rates are well within the range of fees charged in today's marketplace.

We also want to use each of these examples to illustrate how the "average" rate of return and the rate of return you receive on your mutual funds in the market are often not the same (as illustrated in Tables 1 and 2).

Example 1: Positive Market Growth and No Capital Loss

Anna is a civil engineer. She decides to make a single purchase of $10,000 in mutual funds from her broker, Jerry. We are going to follow this purchase over three years (Line **1**, Table 7).

Part 1: Average Rate of Return Without Sales Commission and Mutual Fund Fees

> ### Core Elements
> ☑ Mutual Fund Purchase
>
> ☑ Average Market Rate of Return of 8%
>
> ☑ No Capital Loss
>
> ☑ Impact of Sales Commission and Mutual Fund Fees

We begin with three major assumptions as we follow Anna's money:

1. No initial sales commission of 5%, and no mutual fund fee of 2%.

2. Each year the rate of return fluctuates, but averages 8% over three years.

3. The mutual fund experiences no negative growth (capital loss).

Anna purchases $10,000 of mutual funds (Line **1**, Table 7). At the end of Year 1 (Line **2**, Table 7), we see that Anna's mutual funds have experienced a 9% rate of return resulting in a balance of $10,900.

In Year 2, Anna's mutual funds don't perform quite as well, but still yield a rate of return of 6%. At the end of Year 2 Anna's mutual fund balance is $11,554 (Line **3**, Table 7). At the end of Year 3, with a 9% rate of return, Anna's final mutual fund balance is $12,594 (Line **4**, Table 7). With no capital loss, and without the impact of a sales commission and fees, the actual rate of return achieved by Anna's fund is 8%. (Line **5**, Table 7). Anna feels pleased.

This is the mutual fund performance we all hope for and believe we are getting when we hear about stock market growth averaging 8%

Table 7

Investment Growth *WITHOUT* Sales Load and Mutual Fund Fee

	YEAR 1	
Rate of Return	9%	
Original Mutual Fund Purchase	❶ $ 10,000	
Beginning Balance	$ 10,000	
Investment Gain	$ 900	
Ending Balance	❷ $ 10,900	

Table 8

Investment Growth *WITH* Sales Load and Mutual Fund Fee

	YEAR 1	
Rate of Return	9%	
Original Mutual Fund Purchase	❻ $ 10,000	
Sales Load (5%)	❼ $ (500)	
Beginning Balance	❽ $ 9,500	
Investment Gain	❾ $ 855	
Subtotal	$ 10,355	
Mutual Fund Fee (2%)	❿ $ (207)	
Ending Balance	$ 10,148	

YEAR 2		YEAR 3	Average Rate of Return over 3 Years
6%		9%	8%
$ 0		$ 0	
$ 10,900		$ 11,554	
$ 654		$ 1,040	**Actual Rate of Return over 3 Years**
❸ $ 11,554		❹ $ 12,594	❺ 8%

The actual rates of return presented in Tables 7 and 8 were calculated using the Time Value of Money formula. This equation and the input values for Tables 7 and 8 are included in the Endnotes.

YEAR 2		YEAR 3	Average Rate of Return over 3 Years
6%		9%	8%
$ 0		$ 0	
$ 0		$ 0	The market rate of return averages 8% over 3 years. However, the impact of the sales commission and mutual fund fees reduces the actual rate of return on the mutual fund to 4%.
$ 10,148		$ 10,542	
$ 609		$ 949	
$ 10,757		$ 11,491	
$ (215)		$ (230)	**Actual Rate of Return over 3 Years**
$ 10,542		$ 11,261	⓫ 4%

per year. We lean back in our chair and imagine our money accumulating at this rate for a long time. And we feel secure.

Part 2: The Impact of Sales Commission and Mutual Fund Fees on Average Rate of Return

What we don't understand, though, is the impact of the initial sales commission and the annual mutual fund fee on our mutual fund balance.

Let's follow Anna's money when she pays a one-time 5% sales commission, along with an annual mutual fund fee of 2%. Again, commissions and fees vary across the industry, but these are typical industry values.

So, Anna makes her $10,000 mutual fund purchase (Line **6**, Table 8). She pays $500 as a one-time, front-loaded, mutual fund sales commission (Line **7**, Table 8). The effective starting balance of her account is now reduced to $9,500 (Line **8**, Table 8).

On this initial balance of $9,500, her mutual funds receive a rate of return of 9%. Accordingly, Anna makes a gain of $855 on her mutual fund investment her first year (Line **9**, Table 8). This results in a Year 1 account balance of $10,355. A 2% mutual fund fee of $207 is then deducted from her account balance (Line **10**, Table 8).

When the one-time sales commission and a mutual fund fee are applied to Anna's account, her first year balance is $10,148. Anna has still, technically, earned a 9% rate of return on her money. But the sales commission and fees have resulted in a $752 ($10,900 minus $10,148) *lower* balance as compared to her Year 1 balance ($10,900) when no fees were included (Line **2**, Table 7).

As we track Anna's mutual fund performance over three years, through an average growth of 8%, the erosive power of commissions and fees becomes evident. At the end of three years, despite an average mutual fund performance of 8%, the *actual* growth of Anna's money is **only** 4% (Line ⑪, Table 8). This is half of what Anna believes she is making on her mutual fund account.

This is the powerful and damaging impact sales commissions and mutual fund fees have on investment balance.

The customer-friendly account statements we receive never outline our mutual fund performance in this manner. If they did we'd all likely have a lot more questions and concerns. Fees and charges, while shown on these statements, are often portrayed in ways that minimize our ability to see their direct impact to our bottom line.

This impact occurred even though Anna's mutual funds experienced strong and steady market growth averaging 8% over three years. Anna's mutual funds suffered **no** capital loss during this period, from which they needed to recover.

Our next example illustrates the impact of fees and sales load combined with one year of capital loss but with an average rate of return of 8% over three years.

Example 2: Variable Market Growth and Capital Loss

Mark is a car mechanic. Like Anna from our first case study, Mark decides that he needs to start thinking more about what to do with his money. Mark decides to purchase $10,000 in mutual funds from his friend and broker, Bud.

We are going to follow this single purchase of $10,000 in mutual funds over three years (Line ❶, Table 9).

Fees and charges … are often portrayed in ways that minimize our ability to see their direct impact to our bottom line.

Core Elements:

☑ Mutual Fund Purchase

☑ Average Market Rate of Return of 8%

☑ One Year of Capital Loss

☑ Impact of Sales Commission and Mutual Fund Fees

Part 1: Average Rate of Return Without Sales Commission and Mutual Fund Fees

We start with three assumptions as we track Mark's mutual fund balance:

1. No initial sales commission of 5%, and no mutual fund fee of 2%.

2. Each year the rate of return fluctuates, but averages 8% over three years.

3. The mutual fund experiences **one** year of negative growth (capital loss).

Mark purchases $10,000 of mutual funds (Line ❶, Table 9). By the end of the first year, Mark's mutual funds have experienced a 20% rate of return. This results in a year-end mutual fund balance of $12,000 (Line ❷, Table 9).

In Year 2, Mark's mutual funds yield a rate of return of 18%. At the end of Year 2 Mark's mutual fund balance is $14,160 (Line ❸, Table 9).

In the third year, the stock market does not perform well and Mark's mutual funds experience a negative growth rate of −14%. This is just one year of capital loss in an otherwise strong two-year period of double-digit investment growth.

At the end of Year 3, Mark's final mutual fund balance has dropped to $12,178 (Line ❹, Table 9). The stock market shows an average rate of return over three years of 8%. However, the impact to Mark's mutual fund balance as a result of just **one** year of capital loss is significant. His mutual fund's *actual* rate of return over three years is not the market average of 8% but rather 6.8% (Line ❺, Table 9).

This 6.8% rate of return over three years is still solid growth, but probably not what Mark *thinks* he is making on his mutual funds. If Mark looks at his statements and sees that the average rate of return for Years 1 and 2 were 20% and 18%, he's not as likely to worry about the −14% his funds experienced in Year 3. Those initial double-digit returns are impressive. Like many of us, because Mark does not understand the impact of capital loss, he is likely to believe that his funds are doing better than they actually are.

Part 2: The Impact of Sales Commission and Mutual Fund Fees on Average Rate of Return

Now it's time to follow Mark's money when he pays a one-time 5% sales commission, along with an annual mutual fund fee of 2%.

Once again, Mark makes his $10,000 mutual fund purchase (Line **6**, Table 10). However, this time Mark pays $500 as a one-time, front-loaded, mutual fund sales commission (Line **7**, Table 10). The starting balance of his account is now reduced to $9,500 (Line **8**, Table 10).

On this initial balance of $9,500, Mark's mutual funds receive a first-year rate of return of 20%. Accordingly, Mark makes a gain his first year of $1,900 on his mutual fund investment (Line **9**, Table 10). This results in a Year 1 account balance of $11,400. An annual 2% mutual fund fee of $228 is then deducted from his account balance (Line **10**, Table 10).

The one-time sales commission and a mutual fund fee applied to Mark's account results in a first year balance of $11,172. Mark has still, technically, earned a 20% rate of return on his money over this year. But the impact of the sales commission and fees has resulted in an $828 lower balance ($12,000 minus $11,172) than his mutual fund balance when no fees were included (Line **2**, Table 9).

Each year, Mark pays a mutual fund fee on his account. In his third year, he also experiences one year of negative stock market growth of −14%. The poor market performance in Mark's third year results in a loss of $1,809 to his mutual fund balance.

Table 9 — Investment Growth WITHOUT Sales Load and Mutual Fund Fee

	YEAR 1	
Rate of Return	**20%**	
Original Mutual Fund Purchase	❶ $ 10,000	
Beginning Balance	$ 10,000	
Investment Gain	$2,000	
Ending Balance	❷ $ 12,000	

Table 10 — Investment Growth WITH Sales Load and Mutual Fund Fee

	YEAR 1	
Rate of Return	**20%**	
Original Mutual Fund Purchase	❻ $ 10,000	
Sales Load (5%)	❼ $ (500)	
Beginning Balance	❽ $ 9,500	
Investment Gain	❾ $1,900	
Subtotal	$ 11,400	
Mutual Fund Fee (2%)	❿ $ (228)	
Ending Balance	$ 11,172	

YEAR 2		YEAR 3	Average Rate of Return over 3 Years
18%		−14%	8%
$ 0		$ 0	
$ 12,000		$ 14,160	
$2,160		$ (1,982)	**Actual Rate of Return over 3 Years**
③ $ 14,160		④ $ 12,178	⑤ **6.8%**

The actual rates of return presented in Tables 9 and 10 were calculated using the Time Value of Money formula. This equation and the input values for Tables 9 and 10 are included in the Endnotes.

YEAR 2		YEAR 3	Average Rate of Return over 3 Years
18%		−14%	8%
$ 0		$ 0	The market rate of return averages 8% over 3 years. However, the impact of the one year of capital loss, in combination with the sales commission and mutual fund fees, reduces the actual rate of return on the mutual fund to 2.9%.
$ 0		$ 0	
$ 11,172		$ 12,919	
$ 2,011		$ (1,809)	
$ 13,183		$ 11,110	
$ (264)		$ (222)	**Actual Rate of Return over 3 Years**
$ 12,919		$ 10,888	⑪ **2.9%**

At the end of Year 3, Mark's final mutual fund balance is $10,888. This is only $888 more than the $10,000 Mark started with three years ago (Line **6**, Table 10).

The rate of return for the stock market has averaged 8% over three years. But this is **not** the *actual* rate of return Mark's mutual fund balance has experienced over this same period. Due to the impact of capital loss and fees on his mutual fund balance (Line **11**, Table 10), **Mark has only achieved a 2.9% return on his money.**

This is the effect of one year of capital loss combined with the payment of the sales commission and mutual fund fees.

. . . our most common financial planning vehicles, such as the mutual funds within a 401(k), do not produce predictable outcomes or offer any performance guarantees.

Summing up the Late 20th Century Approach

As we contemplate our late 20th century thinking, we can see that embedded within the financial advice we have consistently received over the past 30 years are the fundamental concepts of **hope, transfer of responsibility,** and **entitlement**. Let's take a closer look.

Hope

Since the inception of the 401(k) and various other qualified plans, we have all been encouraged to believe and hope that investment income from these plans will support us throughout our retirement.

Take a look at Figure 2. Then ask yourself, "What will the value of my 401(k) be in one year? Five years? Ten Years?" That's right, you don't know. Neither does anyone else, including your personal financial advisor.

That's because, as you can see by now, our most common financial planning vehicles, such as the mutual funds within a 401(k), do not produce predictable outcomes or offer any performance guarantees.

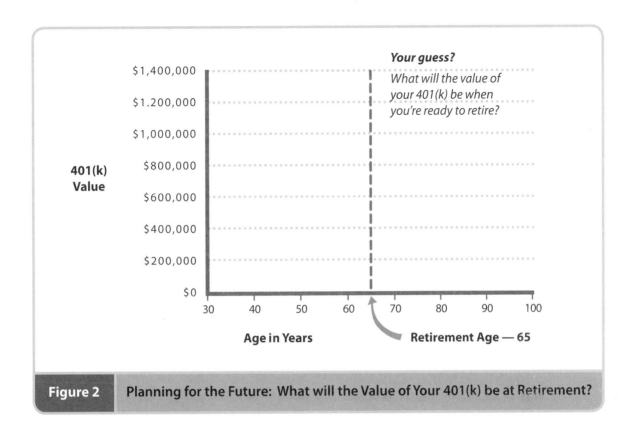

Figure 2 Planning for the Future: What will the Value of Your 401(k) be at Retirement?

We're *hoping* to build a secure financial foundation on money that is at risk in the stock market.

Transfer of Control and Responsibility

When we transfer control and responsibility for our future to others, we place our well-being outside of our own control. We may tell ourselves that others are more knowledgeable or capable. That we can't possibly understand all the nuances of the stock market or financial planning. And we may be right. But what causes us problems is the persistent message that someone else with greater knowledge and power

When we transfer control and responsibility for our future to others, we place our well-being outside of our own control.

will look out for us. This is not true. We are the only ones who can truly act in our best interest. And we need to own this responsibility.

Of course, we can't know everything—especially about all the financial products available to us today. But who says that we are not smart enough to manage our own money?

It's true that most of us are not employed in a job or profession where money is what we "do." For most of us, money is what we earn. Developing expertise in the financial world of stock markets, mutual funds, annuities, and other financial products in addition to our "day job" is often not how we want to spend our time. As a result, we have been relieved to transfer this control and responsibility for our future to our financial planners and advisors, hoping that it will all work out.

When it doesn't work out—when our 401(k) becomes a 201(k)—when it becomes clear that our Social Security income will not be enough to live on, we are the ones with the problem. Not our financial advisors.

Entitlement

Our prevailing late 20th century thinking is that we are entitled to enjoy a secure and enjoyable retirement provided by our companies, government, and financial markets. We are encouraged to believe that our sole responsibility is to simply place money in our qualified plan and the rest will take care of itself. When we are ready to retire, we *should* be able to retire and we *should* have enough money. All at the same time.

We also look to the future and expect Social Security to be there for us. We *hope* that our qualified plan income, supplemented by our Social Security income, will be enough to live well on. However, Social Security was never intended for the general population to live on in retirement for 10, 20, or more years.

We are encouraged to believe that our sole responsibility is to simply place money in our qualified plan and the rest will take care of itself.

We offer this quote from a March 2012 Social Security Administration publication:

> *"…Social Security was never meant to be the only source of income for people when they retire. Social Security replaces about 40 percent of an average wage earner's income after retiring, and most financial advisors say retirees will need 70 percent or more of pre-retirement earnings to live comfortably. To have a comfortable retirement, Americans need much more than just Social Security. They also need private pensions, savings and investments."*[7]

It Doesn't Have to be This Way

It doesn't take a lot to see that the late 20th century paradigm we've been encouraged to embrace—hope, transfer of control and responsibility and entitlement—is not working out so well for a lot of us.

There is a better way.

Consider that there may be a more compelling approach, a more effective way to craft a lifetime financial strategy. We don't have to continue to hand over control and hope for the best. There is a better way.

Let's take a look a different paradigm. One that embraces the challenges we face in the 21st century and moves us toward financial independence.

---

7. "Social Security, Understanding The Benefits," *Social Security Administration*, SSA Publication No. 05-10024, ICN 454930, March 2012.

3

A 21st Century Paradigm

As we move into the 21st century, Suzanne and I want to encourage you to leave behind late 20th century thinking and embrace a new paradigm for an effective lifetime financial strategy. This paradigm is built on the principles of ***knowledge, control, growth*** and ***empowerment***.

Knowledge

From kindergarten through high school everyone is asked what they want to be when they grow up. Our family and community focuses on what jobs or careers we will have over our lifetime. Does anyone ever ask, "And what will you do with the money you earn?"

Unless we seek it out, or are in the extremely unusual position of having someone knowledgeable who takes time to teach us, most of us receive little financial education. So, how can we feel confident to manage our financial life? Well, we weren't born knowing how to add and multiply, someone taught us and we learned. The same is true for our financial education. We need knowledge in order to be able to make decisions in our own best interest. The good news is that this knowledge is readily available.

With financial knowledge you can position yourself to increase your financial security and stability, access your money (and credit) without penalty, and choose how you will finance both planned and unplanned life events.

While no single product or approach is a financial panacea, consider that you have alternatives to chasing a rate of return in your mutual fund, real estate investment, or other financial product. You have the power and ability to look at your life, evaluate your needs and level of risk tolerance, and educate yourself as to what will work best for you.

It's important to identify the core elements that comprise a sustainable lifelong financial strategy. Once we identify what we are looking for in a financial strategy, we can then deliberately select financial products for their strengths while understanding and working within their limitations.

So what characteristics should we look for as part of a lifelong financial strategy? Possible items on our list:

✓ **Security and stability:** we don't want to lose our money.

✓ **Growth:** we want to make money on our money.

✓ **Access to our money without penalty:** we don't want to have to pay just to be able to withdraw or use our money. After all (and we tend to forget this), it is *our* money.

✓ **Fees and service charges:** we don't want to pay unnecessary charges.

✓ **Tax-favorable environment:** we don't want to pay excess taxes.

… consider that you have alternatives to chasing a rate of return in your mutual fund, real estate investment, or other financial product.

Control

In our 21st century paradigm, we want to maintain control over our money. Let's clarify what we mean by control. Clearly, as soon as you take your money out of your mattress and put it somewhere else you lose an element of control over it. It can be stolen, it can be lost. We take this risk because we want to grow our money. So, when we refer to control in the context of this book, we acknowledge that we will be giving up some control as our money will reside somewhere other than our mattress. But what we are talking about here is the ability to place our money into a financial product that allows us to access to our money when we need it (liquidity) without penalty, fees, or service charges.

Is your Money Accessible?

Think about your current financial strategy. You earn hundreds of thousands of dollars or perhaps millions of dollars throughout your lifetime. But in most instances, you have chosen (by default) not to have ready access to it. As a result, you cannot use it to manage changing circumstances and needs. You may have your money in a 401(k) or 529 college savings plan. Perhaps your money is committed to real estate, or resides in a financial product that promises an attractive rate of return, but requires that your money be inaccessible over a fixed time period. For example, in most 401(k) plans, your money can't be withdrawn as long as you are employed by your current employer.

In using these financial products or approaches you have done nothing "wrong." You have simply followed conventional advice to place all your available financial reserves in financial products or vehicles that permit limited access to your money. These products also have variable risk and predetermined penalties if you want to access your money ahead of the scheduled or allowed withdrawal timeline.

When challenged to meet and finance a major unplanned life event (or multiple events) such as a job loss, a health crisis, or the care of an elderly or infirm parent, we need access to our financial reserves.

If our reserves are inaccessible to us, we end up relying upon various lenders, financial institutions, or credit cards for access to cash.

The Joy of Applying for a Loan

Obtaining a loan from a financial institution often starts out with a lot of promises and colorful posters of smiling, contented people. However, obtaining a loan from a financial institution is a process that requires time and a lot of documentation. And despite the best efforts of your loan officer, this process can epitomize the terms "impersonal," "institutional," and "bureaucratic." You jump through hoops to meet the requirements your lender imposes so you can use *their* money to finance your life challenge.

Why do you put yourself through this? Not because you are destitute, far from it. You have been responsible and careful.

You borrow money from others and pay their fees, services charges, and possibly high loan interest because **you don't have access to your own money** *without even* **greater** *penalty.*

This is not the most efficient way to create and grow your wealth over your lifetime. There is a better way.

Growth

To move toward and achieve financial independence means that we must grow our money over time. We want to use specific financial vehicles to achieve compound growth of our money without risk of capital loss, restrictions, or loss of liquidity.

Consider also that we need less money coming through the front door of our financial house if less is going right on out the back door. Money that slips quietly unnoticed out the back door is the money we pay in excess taxes, loan interest, fees, service charges, and through the loss of our investment principal. We are not usually aware of the tremendous impact that these unnoticed or uncontrolled losses have on our long-term financial health.

When we consider growth, we need to consider how the growth of our money is impacted by taxes, fees, service charges, and loss of investment principal.

To move toward and achieve financial independence means that we must grow our money over time.

Empowerment

Any financial plan based on a hoped-for return in the stock market (or any market, for that matter) is not a plan, it's a wish. An effective lifetime financial strategy will work in strong and weak economic times and allow us to mount an effective response to changing and challenging life events.

Any financial plan you can live with and follow for a lifetime ***must also:***

1. be aligned with your values and beliefs about money
2. be based on a comprehensive understanding of your current *overall* financial situation

Any financial plan based on a hoped-for return in the stock market (or any market, for that matter) is not a plan, it's a wish.

3. consider your risk tolerance

4. consider the tax implications of your strategy, current and future

5. systematically address how to build wealth, while also taking into account life's unexpected curves

To accomplish this we need to educate ourselves as to what a healthy financial situation actually looks like.

The Core Elements of an Effective Lifetime Strategy

Despite all the financial jargon out there, the elements of a solid and realizable financial strategy are really not that complicated. It all boils down to the common sense elements we touched on earlier in this chapter.

✓ Security and stability

✓ Growth

✓ Access to our money without penalty (i.e., financial flexibility)

✓ Reduced fees, service charges, and loan interest paid to others

✓ Tax-favored environment

These core elements of a solid financial strategy are listed in Table 11. In Table 11 we also subdivide each core element into the major building blocks you need to have in place to achieve it.

For example, to attain security and stability you need predictable financial results, no loss of your original principal (or capital), and guaranteed cash accumulation (Table 11).

Each Small Step Builds a Long-Term Goal

Remember that achieving financial independence and empowerment is a dynamic process and a journey. You can start out at any age and make a difference. One of the questions Suzanne and I ask ourselves when we want to make a change is simply, "What am I going to do differently today that will make a difference in six months?"

By not expecting that change can be accomplished in a day or perhaps even in six months, we give ourselves room to breathe. We implement little actions each day to move ourselves forward. Small actions, over six months or six years, cover enough distance to reach our goal.

Let's look at the core financial elements that comprise an effective lifetime financial strategy.

> *. . . achieving financial independence and empowerment is a dynamic process and a journey.*

Element 1: Security and Stability

We live in a volatile and ever-changing world. We always have. All those magnificent castles in Europe were not originally built as tourist resorts. They were built for protection and defense against frightening and formidable forces. We have been challenged through human history to balance our desire for security and stability against our desire to see great returns for our effort.

It is true that sometimes in life we need to take large risks to realize a considerable gain. With respect to investments, this is the mantra that the stock market, real estate, and other investors espouse. It is the "no risk, no reward" philosophy.

While it may be a smart move to risk some of your money ***you can afford to lose*** for large returns, the unfortunate reality is that many people place into investments money that they cannot afford to lose. For

Table 11	**Core Elements of a Lifetime Financial Strategy**	
Element 1	Security and Stability	Predictable financial results
		No loss / safe harbor
		Guaranteed cash accumulation
Element 2	Growth	Competitive rate of return
		Flexible contribution limit
Element 3	Access to our Money without Penalty	Liquidity, use, and control
		Guaranteed loan option
		No government involvement
Element 4	Reduced Payments to Others	Reduced loan interest, fees, and service charges
Element 5	Tax-Favored Environment	Reduced tax liability

The cornerstone of your lifelong financial strategy should be a solid foundation of security and stability.

these individuals and their families, when a loss of investment capital does occur, the results can be financially and emotionally devastating.

Remember that ***saving and investing are not the same thing.*** You invest for greater growth at the risk of loss. You save for moderate growth with security, stability, accessibility, and minimal risk of loss.

The cornerstone of your lifelong financial strategy should be a solid foundation of security and stability. To build this, place your money in a financial vehicle where your money (1) experiences predictable growth, (2) is ***not*** subject to capital loss, and in which there is (3) guaranteed cash accumulation. When you are not losing your money, you do not need to make as large a rate of return.

Predictable Financial Results

In Chapter 2, we touched on the power of compound interest and provided an example of growth over time. With compound interest you earn interest on your original principal as well as on any other interest you may have accumulated.

When you place money in a vehicle that harnesses the power of compound interest, you grow your money at a steady, predictable, and sustainable rate. The sooner you start to save, the greater the benefit of compound interest.

No Loss / Safe Harbor

When we lose our initial principal in an investment, it stands to reason that we want to make up this loss sometime in the future. We often hear the standard advice that when we are young we can afford investments with greater risk.

Why should we lose money at any age for any reason? In fact, losing money when we are young is one of our most expensive losses because we have lost the time that this money would have had to compound.

We can get caught in the cycle of choosing high-risk investments that promise enticing rates of return. If we lose our capital or don't achieve the promised rate of return, instead of reconsidering our financial strategy, we invest more money into another high-risk product. We want to believe our nerve and willingness to take risks will eventually be rewarded with a windfall that more than makes up for our losses.

This approach is akin to sitting at the slot machines, feeding in dollar after dollar, waiting for the jackpot. Of course, you cannot rule

> "Compound interest is the eighth wonder of the world. He, who understands it, earns it . . . he who doesn't . . . pays it."
>
> —ALBERT EINSTEIN
> (ATTRIBUTED)

out the possibility of a big win. But this approach is hardly one you want to use to anchor a lifetime financial strategy.

Guaranteed Cash Accumulation

Financial security and stability build when your money accumulates predictably and reliably over time. When you grow your money and have guaranteed accumulation, you are better prepared to manage and weather both planned and unplanned life events.

Element 2: Growth

Competitive Rate of Return

Hope is important, but it should not be your only companion when you map out a financial plan.

One of the reasons we all look at investment vehicles as a place to put our money is because we want to grow our money at the fastest possible rate. We want big returns. We have all heard the story of the hot stock tip that paid out big time. We look at the ascending jagged edge of the stock market graph and see the underlying upward trend. We want to catch that upward growth, "ride the wave," and experience what it is like to see those heady returns.

At some point in your financial life you need to decide whether you want to chase a return or create a strategy.

True, the two concepts are not mutually exclusive. But remember that a rate of return usually involves an investment whose outcome you cannot predict. You are *not* in control of the results. You are *hoping* for a big return. Hope is important, but it should not be your only companion when you map out a financial plan.

Moderate, predictable growth combined with a 'no loss' strategy can carry you much further in the long-term than you might think. If you are in doubt, refer back to Tables 4 through 6.

Remember that the effect of just one period of capital loss at any point over the investment period can have a long-lasting negative impact on your wealth.

Flexible Contribution Limit (versus a Defined Contribution Limit)

When you are growing your wealth, you do not want to be limited as to the amount of money you can save. Some years you will have more money to place into your financial reserve and other years you won't. What you don't want is someone else or government regulations to direct how much money you can save.

We need to consider the capacity of our financial vehicle to accept our money. Most people don't consider this when analyzing the effectiveness of their financial strategy.

Element 3: Access to Your Money without Penalty

Liquidity, Use, and Control[1]

In accounting terms, *liquidity* means that you can convert an asset to cash in less than 12 months. What we mean when we talk about liquidity is that you can access your cash within two weeks to a month. When you can achieve this type of liquidity with your financial strategy, you position yourself to take advantage of a financial opportunity or be able to pay an emergency expense.

Use means that you have the money available for what you require or desire without restrictions. For example, when you take out a car loan or a home loan from the bank, the funds are restricted to this

---

1. Donald. L. Blanton, *Your Circle of Wealth* (Covington, Louisiana, Mele Printing, 2004), page 27.

particular use. If you purchase a certificate of deposit (CD) and need to access the money before the term is up, you are charged a penalty for early withdrawal.

Control means that you are solely able to determine the use of your money. If you want to change the location of your money, spend it, loan it, or invest it, there are no penalties, no age restrictions, and no one to tell you that you can't do what you want to do.

These three factors—liquidity, use, and control of your money—are critical to your ability to withstand a financial crisis, a job loss, change in health, or family emergency. Unfortunately, when these types of crises occur, lending institutions will typically not loan you money. When you need cash (and regular cash flow) to pay your bills, it's not a good time to realize that you don't have easy access to cash.

When you need cash (and regular cash flow) to pay your bills, it's not a good time to realize that you don't have easy access to cash.

Access to Cash if Life Throws You a Curve Ball

Ask yourself how much of your money you could convert to cash within a month. To access your financial reserves would you face withdrawal penalties, fees, or service charges, or need to rely on a sale of an asset (such as in real estate)? How might you cope with a sudden change in your life? When you need cash, you can be forced to sell an asset whether it's a good time to sell or not.

The unfortunate truth is that most of us have limited liquidity, use, and control over our own money.

Who knows what the future will bring? An effective lifetime financial strategy positions us to have the power to choose our response to changing life conditions.

The unfortunate truth is that most of us have limited liquidity, use, and control over our own money.

Guaranteed Loan Option: the Freedom to Access your Money

Each financial institution has its own set of rules and criteria for lending money. Since you are asking to use someone else's money, you do not have control over the process the lender uses to decide whether or not they will let you borrow their money.

When we borrow money from a financial institution there are three major considerations: 1) the interest rate that your lender will charge you to use their money; 2) your qualification, that is, whether such factors as your income, job history, and credit score (plus other criteria) will meet the lender's approval; and, 3) the establishment of a structured loan repayment schedule.

A solid financial plan takes into account the reality that you will likely need to borrow money to finance both planned life events (such as a car, college, a wedding, etc.) and unplanned events (like a job loss or health crisis).

A strong financial plan also creates a reserve where the money you save can be accessed and borrowed. When you allow for this type of access to your own money, you may essentially eliminate seeking loans from other people or institutions. Borrowing from your own financial reserve and then replenishing this reserve (similar to how you would pay back a bank loan) is another way to gain control over your financial life.

No Government Involvement: Should the Government Manage your Money?

With qualified plans, including your 401(k), the government can change the rules at any time. The rules can and do keep changing to fit the time, a new political agenda, or whatever the government wants to do.

Changing regulations can inadvertently penalize the folks who have made every effort to do the right thing.

Changing regulations can inadvertently penalize the folks who have made every effort to do the right thing.

Choose a vehicle that is as free of government involvement as possible to form the bedrock of your financial life. You don't want to be regulated as to how much you can contribute to your savings. You also don't want someone or some government agency determining when you can withdraw your money, how much, and under what conditions. You deserve the freedom to choose how your money moves and when to access it.

Element 4: Reduced Payments to Others

Many of us pay a large amount of money (in the form of loan interest and fees) to others for the privilege of borrowing their money. We pay loan interest on our cars, homes, and other loans. If we carry a monthly balance on our credit cards, we can be paying an interest rate as high as 29.99% or more.

We also pay other people to help us manage our money. At our financial institutions, we pay ATM fees, debit card fees, account maintenance, and transaction fees. In our qualified plans, we pay transfer fees, paper fees, and service fees, to name but a few.

When you eliminate many of the fees and service charges banks and other lenders charge, this money stays in your financial system.

Reduced Loan Interest, Fees, and Service Charges

Any approach we choose for our lifelong strategy should allow us to reduce the amount of loan interest, fees, and service charges we pay. By reducing loan interest, fees, and service charges, we decrease how much money we let leak out of our financial system. Consequently, we grow our wealth faster. Think about filling a child's inflatable swimming pool. When there are leaks, it takes a lot longer to fill the pool and it does not stay full. When you find and seal the leaks, it takes a lot less water to fill the pool and it stays full.

When you eliminate many of the fees and service charges banks and other lenders charge, this money stays in your financial system. Over time, the effect of reducing these financial leaks can be significant. Just as with our swimming pool metaphor. Once you eliminate the small but steady leaks in your financial system and capture or reduce the outflow, your money stays with you. You don't have to earn, or grow, as much money over your lifetime if you're not losing it.

Element 5: Tax-Favored Environment

With a little thought and planning, we can ensure that we pay the taxes we owe, but not more.

We believe in paying taxes. They support our community, pay our educators, police, fire fighters, and fund the local, regional, and federal programs that make our society strong. We need an infrastructure of roads, utilities, military, and other services to ensure a minimum standard of living and security. And we need to support members of our society who need Social Security, Medicare, and Medicaid. All these programs and needs are supported with our contributions and tax dollars.

That said, we only want to pay taxes on our income *once*, not over and over again. With a little thought and planning, we can ensure that we pay the taxes we owe, but *not more.*

A solid strategy should include a tax-favored environment for our money.

Looking into the Crystal Ball

We do know with relative assurance that controlling our future taxable income is important to our financial well-being.

None of us can know for certain what the future will bring. We *do* know with relative assurance that *controlling* our future taxable income is important to our financial well-being.

How can we say this?

Because in most cases, the largest amount of tax we pay is referenced to income: how much of our income is taxable and at what rate. By strategically managing our taxable income, our cash flow, our taxable expenses, and consequently, the money we pay in taxes, we end up able to keep and use more of that money.

Our ability to save in a tax-favored environment that we control can be critical to growing our long-term wealth in the 21st century.

Toward Financial Independence in the 21st Century

There are a lot of financial products in the marketplace. Each financial tool or product is designed with a specific target goal or purpose in mind. The problems arise when we use a product designed for one purpose (e.g., security) but want a result that the product was not designed to achieve (e.g., a high rate of return).

We might also expect a product primarily designed for growth, which contains a higher level of risk, to operate also as a savings product. It is this type of unclear thinking that we have been faced with when we hear people use the erroneous expression, "saving for retirement in a 401(k)."

We've listed some of the more familiar financial products and choices in Table 12. Each of the financial products you see in this table come with characteristics related to its risk, rate of return, tax liability, liquidity, and predictability.

When we look at the list of some of the more familiar financial products in Table 12, it's apparent that there are more financial products available to us than mutual funds and real estate.

While no one single financial product can fulfill everyone's needs, there are financial products in the marketplace that can serve as a cornerstone of a lifelong financial plan.

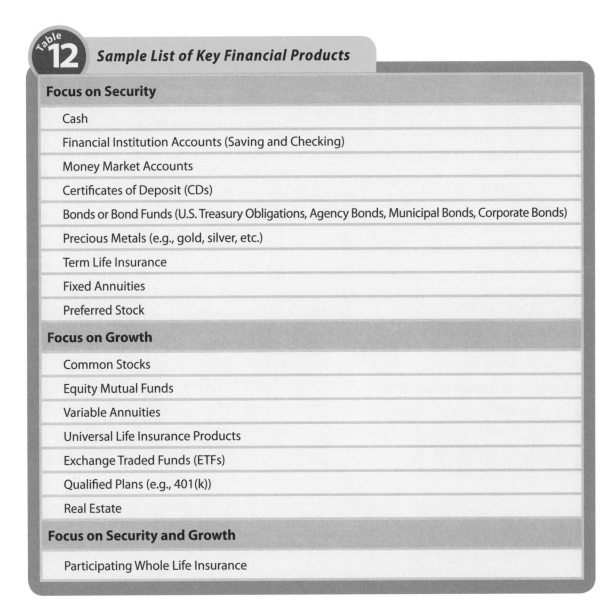

Table 12 Sample List of Key Financial Products

Focus on Security

Cash

Financial Institution Accounts (Saving and Checking)

Money Market Accounts

Certificates of Deposit (CDs)

Bonds or Bond Funds (U.S. Treasury Obligations, Agency Bonds, Municipal Bonds, Corporate Bonds)

Precious Metals (e.g., gold, silver, etc.)

Term Life Insurance

Fixed Annuities

Preferred Stock

Focus on Growth

Common Stocks

Equity Mutual Funds

Variable Annuities

Universal Life Insurance Products

Exchange Traded Funds (ETFs)

Qualified Plans (e.g., 401(k))

Real Estate

Focus on Security and Growth

Participating Whole Life Insurance

In Table 13, Suzanne and I have compared the financial products listed in Table 12 against the core elements of an effective lifetime strategy that we have discussed in this chapter.

Table 13 — Key Strengths and Limitations of Common Financial Products

Desired Financial Result		Cash	Financial Institution Accounts (Saving/ Checking)	Certificates of Deposit (CDs)	Bonds or Bond Funds[1]	Precious Metals (e.g., gold, silver)	Term Life Insurance	Fixed Annuities
Security and Stability	Predictable Financial Results	✓	✓	✓	✓		✓	✓
	No Capital Loss / Safe Harbor	✓	✓	✓[2]	✓[2]			✓
	Guaranteed Cash Accumulation	✓	✓	✓[2]	✓[2]			✓
Growth	Competitve Rate of Return		✓	✓	✓	✓		✓
	Flexible Contribution Limit	✓	✓	✓	✓	✓		✓
Access to our Money without Penalty	Liquidity, Use and Control	✓	✓	✓		✓		
	Guaranteed Loan Option							
	No Government Involvement	✓	✓	✓	✓	✓	✓	
Tax-Favored	Tax-Deferred Growth							✓
	Tax-Free Death Benefit						✓	
	Tax-Deductible Contributions							

Notes

1. The interest on municipal bonds is tax-free.   2. Applicable if held to maturity.

	Financial Product Focus on Growth								Financial Product Focus on Security and Growth
Preferred Stock	Common Stocks	Equity Mutual Funds	Variable Annuities	Universal Life Insurance Products	Exchange Traded Funds	Qualified Plans (e.g., 401(k))	Real Estate		Participating Whole Life Insurance
									✓
									✓
									✓
✓	✓	✓	✓	✓	✓	✓	✓		✓
✓	✓	✓	✓	✓	✓		✓		✓
✓	✓	✓		✓	✓				✓
									✓
✓	✓	✓		✓	✓		✓		✓
			✓	✓		✓	✓		✓
				✓					✓
						✓			

General Comment: The purpose of this table is to provide a broad overview and comparison of financial product characteristics. However, due to the complexity and variety of financial products available, the features of specific products may vary slightly from the general characteristics outlined in Table 13.

Peruse Table 13. As you look at this table you will notice a surprising fact—participating whole life insurance has tremendous financial strengths.

This surprised us when we first looked at it, too. What Suzanne and I have learned is that **when designed correctly**, there are *powerful* financial benefits to a participating whole life insurance policy *used as a financial tool.*

"living benefits" …provide a financial resource for you to use and enjoy during your lifetime.

The Power of Whole Life Insurance as a Financial Tool

Whether you are familiar with insurance or not, as you study Table 13 you might notice that many of the advantages of participating whole life insurance designed as a financial tool are "living benefits." In other words, they provide a financial resource for you to use and enjoy *during* your lifetime. These living benefits are present in addition to the tax-free legacy of the death benefit that will be left to your beneficiaries. Unfortunately, it is the death benefit, not the financial power of the living benefits that people tend to focus on when they think of life insurance.

Participating whole life insurance can function as a simple and powerful tool by operating as a secure savings plan, which becomes part of your lifetime financial strategy. When you use a custom-designed participating whole life insurance policy as part of a financial strategy, you are shifting the location of your money. You are moving your money out of a volatile investment vehicle (such as mutual funds in the stock market) as the depository for all your money, and placing it in a more stable location. One which eliminates the risk of capital loss and takes advantage of the power of compound interest.

The security of participating whole life insurance can form the cornerstone of your financial strategy in the 21st century. The foundation of this strategy is built on predictable results, financial control, and lifetime access to your cash without penalty.

As you look at Table 13, a natural question emerges: *"If participating whole life insurance works so well, why is it that this powerful financial tool isn't well known or used by the general public?"*

We're still searching to find a comprehensive answer to this question. A partial answer might be that there are powerful forces in place to keep the stock market at the forefront of our financial thinking. Two of these forces are the "mutual fund industry" and Wall Street. Another factor might simply be our loyalty to the late 20th century paradigm that tells us we must be in the market and "buy and hold" to see our money grow.

Charting a New Course

In this book, Suzanne and I want to introduce you to the concept and the practice of using a custom-designed participating whole life insurance policy as a financial tool. ***A properly designed participating whole life policy can function as a simple and powerful financial tool that will work in strong and weak economic times.*** It can be used as a stand-alone strategy or in combination with other investment vehicles and approaches.

It's a concept and a practice that has been around for a very long time. It's a financial staple of the wealthy and is currently standard business practice for executives, corporations, and banks.

You don't have to accept the late 20th century paradigm which encourages us to transfer control and responsibility of our financial lives to others. We don't need to hope that it will all work out if we just shut our eyes and believe. That approach may have worked for Dorothy in the Wizard of Oz but it is not a solid strategy as we face the 21st century.

You can set yourself on a different path.

You can set yourself on a different path. There's nothing stopping you from using a participating whole life policy as the cornerstone of your financial plan while investing in the stock market or other assets.

As we explore the power of this financial tool, you'll see that you can use a participating whole life policy as a savings vehicle, credit facility, college savings plan and a supplemental retirement plan. With this financial tool as the foundation of your lifetime strategy, you can optimize the efficiency of your money while achieving financial independence.

So let's get started!

4

An Insurance Primer

Most of us view insurance as a necessary expense. We buy insurance because we have been taught this is how we can protect something that matters to us such as our car, our house, or our health. Or we buy life insurance in order to create financial protection for our family and those we love when we die.

It is time to expand our understanding of the world of insurance.

A properly designed participating whole life insurance policy offers powerful benefits as the cornerstone of a lifelong financial strategy.

How is this possible? To find out we need to develop a basic understanding and knowledge of this product and how it operates.

The insurance world has its industry jargon. However, the basic components of life insurance and the insurance industry are not hard to understand. And the benefits of comprehending these components are enormous. By gaining this knowledge, you can set yourself on a different path—one enabling you and your family to reach a level of financial independence, peace of mind, and safety that you might never have thought possible.

To take this road, you'll need an open mind and a willingness to get familiar with some basic insurance information. So let's begin.

It is time to expand our understanding of the world of insurance.

How Insurance Companies are Structured

Insurance companies are organized as either publicly traded or private mutual companies. Let's take a look at each of these company structures.

Publicly Traded Insurance Company

A publicly traded company is owned by the stockholders (or shareholders). Its shares are registered securities for sale to the general public, typically through a stock exchange. These organizations are called stock companies or legal reserve stock companies. Under this type of company organization the stockholders, *not policy owners,* share in profits. Stocks and/or bonds may be offered to the public for purchase, and new issues may be offered to raise capital.

Private Mutual Insurance Company

Mutual companies are private insurance companies owned by the policy owners. Mutual companies may issue participating policies that allow policy owners to share in dividends, when declared.

Unlike publicly traded stock-based companies, private mutual companies have no outside stockholders to share in the profits. Consequently, the private mutual insurance company is not subject to short-term performance demands of the stock market or the need to show quarterly or annual earnings to satisfy shareholder needs.

The Company Owners are the Policy Owners

With respect to the whole life insurance policy, mutual companies are able to keep more clearly focused on the benefits for their policy owners because of the singularity of their stated mission, which is simply the long-term interests of the policy owners.

Insurance Companies and Banks— What's the Difference?

The safety and security of your life insurance policy depends on the insurer from which you purchase your policy. So it makes sense to start with the big picture about insurance companies and understand how they are different from banks.

How Banks Operate

It's a rare person who spends much time thinking about how banks and financial institutions make their money. But we can learn quite a lot if we take a moment to consider this. It has direct implications for us as we develop a financial strategy designed to be effective over our lifetime.

Fractional reserve banking

Banks in the U.S. operate using fractional reserve banking. This is a practice in which commercial banks are required to keep only a fraction of the money deposited with them as reserves. For example, if the reserve

... banks make their money by loaning our money back to us.

requirement is 10%, and you deposit $100 in your bank, your bank will then lend out $90 (keeping $10 for reserve) of your $100 deposit.

So, banks make their money by *loaning our money back to us*. In the process of loaning us our money they collect interest and fees on the money they lend.

The fractional reserve system works because, usually, the total amount of withdrawals is offset by deposits made at the same time. You can see how the bank is critically dependent upon borrowers making their loan payments regularly and on time. Another critical aspect of the fractional reserve system is consumer confidence. When people's confidence in the banking system is shaken a "bank run" may occur. This is a situation in which many people rush to withdraw their money at the same time due to their concern about the safety and accessibility of their money.

Tier one assets (liquid cash reserve)

Banks rely on a core liquid cash reserve referred to as Tier One Capital (or Assets) as a measure of their financial strength. Tier One Capital consists of safe *liquid* assets such as cash, precious metals, loans from the federal government, demand deposits, short term notes, and bank-owned life insurance (BOLI).[1]

Tier One Capital is the financial cushion that the bank depends upon during periods of adversity.

Regulators *do not* allow equity investments—investments in the stock market—in Tier One Capital as they are considered too volatile.

Barry Dyke, author of *The Pirates of Manhattan*, made the following observations: *"Bankers have wholeheartedly embraced*

---

1. "Cash Value Life Insurance: A Cornerstone Asset of a Bank," insurancenewsnet.com, November 24, 2008, http://www.insurancenewsnet.com/print.asp?a=top_lh&id+100927 (accessed August 15, 2010).

high cash value life insurance as a safe economic power tool and have found the product to be healthy for the bottom line. . . . The CEO [of a Midwestern bank] confessed to [his/her] advisor that the bank-owned life insurance was the bank's best performing asset." [2]

So, one of the principal measures of financial stability and strength for a bank is the size of the liquid financial reserve they possess which includes cash, precious metals, and *participating whole life insurance.*

How Insurance Companies Operate

Insurance companies operate within unique legal requirements and regulatory structures that are very different from banks. This has helped them avoid many of the ills that plague the banking industry. Insurance executives are aware that they must invest the premiums of their customers prudently because someday the death benefit will have to be paid.

Insurance companies maintain reserves for the payment of losses or claims and expenses. Reserves are funds created for the purpose of paying anticipated death claims under insurance policies. In other words, insurance companies are required by law to maintain reserves that are set aside to pay future claims.

It's interesting to note that mutual life insurance companies are among the largest and most consistently long-lasting financial institutions. In fact, many American life insurance companies in business today trace their roots to the early part of the 19th century. During the past 150 years, we have witnessed a cycle of boom and bust for the banking industry. But the insurance industry has maintained a tradition of paying its claims through economic good and bad times. This legacy continues today. This is why financial professionals are able to recommend participating whole life

. . . insurance companies are required by law to maintain reserves that are set aside to pay future claims.

2. Barry James Dyke, *Pirates of Manhattan* (Portsmouth, New Hampshire, 555 Publishing, 2007), page 149.

insurance, among other insurance industry products, for its safe and predictable financial results.

The Life Insurance Policy—An Overview

In its simplest form, life insurance is a legal agreement between the policy owner and the life insurance company. The policy owner agrees to make periodic payments to the insurance company. In turn, they agree to pay a sum of money, a "death benefit," to a beneficiary (or beneficiaries) of your choosing if the person who is insured dies.

The money received from the death benefit assists in the economic stability of family members at the time of death. Often, a tax-free death benefit replaces lost income which can then be used to pay the mortgage, provide for education, and meet other expenses.

You can also buy life insurance on someone other than yourself, as long as you have an "insurable interest" in this person. That is to say, the owner of the insurance policy (the policy owner) must have a clear economic interest in the continued life of the insured person in order to be able to buy insurance on someone other than themselves.

Businesses and corporations routinely purchase and own life insurance policies on key personnel as part of their business succession or continuity planning strategy.

Insurance companies offer two basic types of life insurance in various forms: term life insurance and permanent life insurance.

Term Life Insurance

Term life insurance protects you for a specific "term." Term life insurance can be purchased to cover different time spans such as 10-, 20-, and 30-year periods. Term life insurance pays a death benefit *if* the person insured dies within the term covered by the insurance.

Term life insurance does not have a savings component (or cash value) and you cannot cash it in.

Term life insurance premiums are level (i.e., they don't increase) over the initial period of the insurance. Once the initial period is reached (i.e., 20 years in a 20-year term policy), if the policy is renewable, you may continue to pay the premium for another period (usually year by year) at the premium rate stated in the policy without providing health information. However, the renewed term life insurance policy will cost more and more each year. At some point in time, this type of policy may become too expensive to continue.

Permanent Life Insurance

Permanent life insurance refers to life insurance policies that do not have a defined term and which combine a death benefit with a "cash value" component. Cash value is the equity component of the insurance policy, meaning that if you collapse the policy you will receive this amount of money.

The two main types of permanent life insurance are universal life and whole life insurance. Let's take a brief look at these two types of permanent life insurance.

Universal Life Insurance

Universal life insurance, Variable Universal, and Equity Index Universal life insurance are all insurance vehicles that *share* security products. Universal insurance products combine permanent life insurance policy characteristics with investment products.

Universal life policies are tied to an interest rate or the anticipated performance of an investment vehicle.

As the owner of a Universal life, Variable Universal, or Equity Index Universal policy you need to make sure that your cash value accumulation, via premiums and internal growth, is enough to cover the monthly insurance and policy expenses. These expenses are recalculated periodically and increase each year as your probability of dying increases and the cost of insurance goes up.

If your cash value is not growing at a fast enough rate, monthly insurance and policy expenses will use up the cash value and your policy could lapse. This can happen even when you make your premium payments on time.

Since these life insurance products are dependent upon interest rates or some other variable market, they inherently harbor more risk than insurance policies that do not have these characteristics.

Whole Life Insurance

Whole life insurance is the traditional type of permanent life insurance. You pay fixed premiums annually or monthly. The policy endures for the entire life of the insured and is not subject to the whims of the market. The performance and value of a whole life insurance policy are not correlated to the stock market. And it is guaranteed by the insurer. ***This means that the cash value and death benefit are not affected by declining markets.***

As long as premiums are paid, the policy is guaranteed to continue and your cash value will increase. The living benefits of whole life insurance make it one of the most valuable and flexible financial planning tools available.

In this book, we are dealing specifically with the application of permanent, participating whole life insurance as a financial tool and as the cornerstone of a lifetime financial strategy. (The term participating

In this book, we are dealing specifically with the application of permanent, participating whole life insurance as a financial tool and as the cornerstone of a lifetime financial strategy.

is used to describe any insurance policy that pays a dividend to its policy owners).

Now let's review some key components of whole life insurance in greater detail.

Basic Components of a Participating Whole Life Policy

The whole life insurance policy is a private, legal contract between the policy owner, the insured, and the insurance company. As the policy owner, you enter into a defined arrangement with the insurance company. Very specific contractual elements protect you.

Whole life insurance offers level premiums and life insurance protection for as long as you live. All you have to do is pay premiums as required to keep the policy in-force.

Whole life insurance can also provide what are referred to as "living benefits." Living benefits are provided by the accumulation of cash value *and* the death benefit inside the whole life insurance policy.

Living benefits provide a financial resource for you to use and enjoy during your lifetime.

Living benefits provide a financial resource for you to use and enjoy *during your lifetime*. For example, with whole life insurance it is possible to take policy loans, use the life insurance policy for collateral on bank or other loans, or use the policy for retirement income, cash withdrawals, and more.

It is these living benefits that can be used to develop the cornerstone of a lifelong financial strategy.

Three guarantees form the foundation of a whole life policy: (1) level premiums, (2) cash value and (3) death benefit. Let's take a look at each element.

Premiums, Cash Value, and Death Benefit

The premium is the money you pay the insurance company on a regular, periodic basis to obtain a specific amount of insurance. "Base premium" refers to the basic premium you must pay to keep a whole life policy in-force. The base premium does not increase (remains level) over the entire life of the policy. Usually, the policy owner pays the premium.

Whole life insurance is contracted to last for the insured's whole (entire) life. The premiums create a growing cash asset, referred to as the policy's "cash value." The policy's cash value is a living benefit. It is the "savings" portion of a whole life policy. Participating whole life policies have a guaranteed cash value and non-guaranteed dividends. The guaranteed cash value is the amount in the policy if the company were never to pay dividends.

How the cash value of your whole life policy is calculated varies depending upon the particular policy and insurance company. You can access the cash value you have accumulated, at any time and for any reason, generally with no penalty or tax liabilities. You can use the cash value in a participating whole life policy for any purpose you choose. Typical uses for the cash value include:

✓ Education expenses

✓ Capital for business

✓ Provision of emergency funds

✓ Collateral for a bank loan

✓ Policy premium payment or loan interest

✓ Supplemental retirement income

A participating whole life policy has a guaranteed death benefit. The death benefit provided by the policy is disbursed to beneficiaries when the insured dies.

Dividend Payments

Insurance dividends are paid on participating whole life insurance policies. Dividend payments are set annually by a mutual insurance company's board of directors and are not guaranteed, although most mutual insurance companies have paid out these dividends every year for well over 100 years.

Insurance companies use different methods to calculate dividends. In general, they base the dividend determination on the company's portfolio performance, mortality claims experience, and expense control. Once dividends are paid, they become part of the cash value within your policy. They cannot be lost or arbitrarily deducted out of your policy in the future. Dividends also grow tax-deferred while in the policy.

There are some specific ways you can use dividends. You can:

- ✓ have your dividends paid to you in cash
- ✓ use dividends to reduce your premium
- ✓ use dividends to purchase additional insurance
- ✓ choose to allow your dividends to accumulate with interest
- ✓ pay back an existing policy loan
- ✓ pay back just the interest on an existing policy loan

Paid-up Additions

Paid-up additions (also referred to as PUAs) are additional amounts of fully paid-up life insurance that you can add to your existing whole life insurance policy. These extra amounts of additional insurance are just like your existing whole life insurance policy: they have their own guaranteed cash value and non-guaranteed dividend and death benefit.

Upon first glance, it seems a little odd to add additional insurance to your existing participating whole life insurance policy each year. The question that springs to mind is, "why bother?"

The short answer is that by buying these extra amounts of additional life insurance you are able to increase the amount of money that you put into your policy and consequently, you increase the amount of money growing inside your policy. Equally important, you increase the death benefit creating greater financial protection for your family.

Since paid-up additions are additional amounts of life insurance, they earn their own dividends. These dividends are then added to those paid to your existing policy. When you use the paid-up additions feature you are adding extra savings into your policy upon which dividends are then paid. Since you have more death benefit in your existing whole life policy, you receive a larger dividend payment. It's a circular increasing benefit. The more paid-up additions, the larger your cash value and the more death benefit you have inside your policy.

When you use paid-up additions you gain incredible flexibility in how you operate your policy.

When you use paid-up additions you gain incredible flexibility in how you operate your policy. In any year, you must make the basic premium payment to keep the policy in-force. However, you can also choose to pay additional premium amounts to purchase paid-up additions. This gives you financial flexibility as to where to put your extra savings when you have them.

Your policy can also be designed so that your base policy dividend payments are used to purchase paid-up additions. You can make this a standard option of your policy design so that each year, your declared dividends automatically purchase more paid-up additions.

Policy Loans

When you take a loan against your policy you borrow from the insurance company but you do not actually remove any money from your policy.

What you are doing when you borrow against your policy is taking a loan using the financial reserves of the insurance company. The cash value and death benefit in your policy act as collateral for the loan.

Since you have not actually withdrawn money from your policy, the money in your policy continues to compound and grow while you have a loan against it. This is an important strength of a participating whole life contract. You continue to earn dividends on the death benefit inside your policy even though you have taken a loan against the policy.

As you repay your policy loan, the insurance company incrementally releases the lien against the cash value of the policy.

You may repay your loan on any schedule you feel comfortable with, creating *your own* repayment terms. Best of all, the loans you receive are not taxable income.

If the loan is not repaid when the insured person dies, the outstanding loan balance (plus interest) is subtracted from the death benefit.

When you take a loan against your participating whole life policy you need to treat it as though you had obtained a loan from your local financial institution. Your responsibilities are all the same. Remember that regardless of the financial vehicle you choose to use, good stewardship and responsibility are critical to its strong performance.

You may repay your loan on any schedule you feel comfortable with, creating your own repayment terms.

Policy Loans versus Policy Withdrawals

The policy owner has two options to access the cash value inside his or her policy. The policy owner can either take a policy loan, as previously discussed, or alternatively, take a withdrawal.

When you withdraw money from your life insurance policy, you do not incur loan interest. However, if you withdraw more money from your policy that you paid in premiums, tax could be due on your withdrawal.

Withdrawing money from your policy decreases the cash value, death benefit, and the total capacity of the policy. In contrast, policy loans decrease the cash value and death benefit but the *capacity of the policy is not reduced.*

Policy capacity

Policy capacity is an important concept. When you take a withdrawal of $50,000 from your participating whole life policy, you reduce the capacity of the policy. What this means is that you, as the policy owner, cannot put back the $50,000 into the policy at a later date as a lump sum. Withdrawing money is equivalent to reducing the size of the bucket. You still have your whole life insurance policy; you pay your base premium and have flexibility with your paid-up additions. But should you need a place to put $50,000 you cannot put it back in your policy.

Table 14 compares the impact of taking $50,000 as a withdrawal versus a policy loan.

Which is better—policy loans or withdrawals?

And the answer is . . . it depends. If the policy owner does not foresee that he or she would want to return the $50,000 to the policy in the future then a withdrawal might be the best answer.

However, if the policy owner wants to retain the option of placing the $50,000 back into the policy, then a policy loan is the best answer. For example, should the policy owner want to fund a major purchase, such as a car, the loan option is probably best. Because over time, the owner wants to refill the policy with the amount borrowed and keep the policy capacity. Policy loans also

Table 14 — The Impact of Policy Loans versus Policy Withdrawals

Policy Parameters	Policy Loan	Policy Withdrawal
Accessible Cash[1]	$50,000	$50,000
Tax Consequence	No tax consequence	Variable—*if you withdraw more money from your policy than you paid in premiums, there could be tax due on your withdrawals.*
Cash Value	Reduced by $50,000	Reduced by $50,000
Death Benefit	Reduced by $50,000	Reduced by $50,000
Loan Interest	Loan interest accrues	No loan interest
Unpaid Loan Interest	Unpaid loan interest reduces the cash value and the death benefit	No unpaid loan interest
Policy Capacity	Policy capacity unchanged	Policy capacity reduced

Note

1. Cash value amount presented in this table is an arbitrary amount chosen for illustrative purposes only.

allow the policy's extra capacity to be available should unexpected income be received, such as an inheritance.

Policy loans maintain greater financial flexibility for the policy owner. Consequently, we focus on the use of policy loans instead of withdrawals to illustrate the flexibility of the participating whole life policy as a financial tool.

Policy loans maintain greater financial flexibility for the policy owner.

Policy Riders

Riders are additional contractual options you can have added to your life insurance policy with additional cost. These options allow you to increase your insurance coverage or limit the coverage set down by the policy.

Guaranteed insurability rider

A guaranteed insurability rider allows you to purchase additional separate whole life insurance policies, at specified ages of the insured's life, without proof of medical insurability. With this rider in place, the insured could purchase additional life insurance policies even if his or her health has deteriorated.

Waiver of premium rider

The waiver of premium rider is another common choice among policy owners. This rider guarantees that if the policy owner becomes permanently disabled, the premiums for the policy will continue to be paid by the insurance company to age 65. With this rider in place, the policy will continue to provide increased cash value, net death benefit, and dividends as if the policy owner had not become disabled.

Accelerated death benefit rider

This rider allows for the pre-payment of a portion of the policy's death benefit when the insured is terminally ill or has an injury that will result in death within 12 months.

Policy Ownership

It is possible to own an insurance policy on someone else. In other words, while you can certainly own a whole life policy on yourself, many individuals own one (or several) policies on other people,

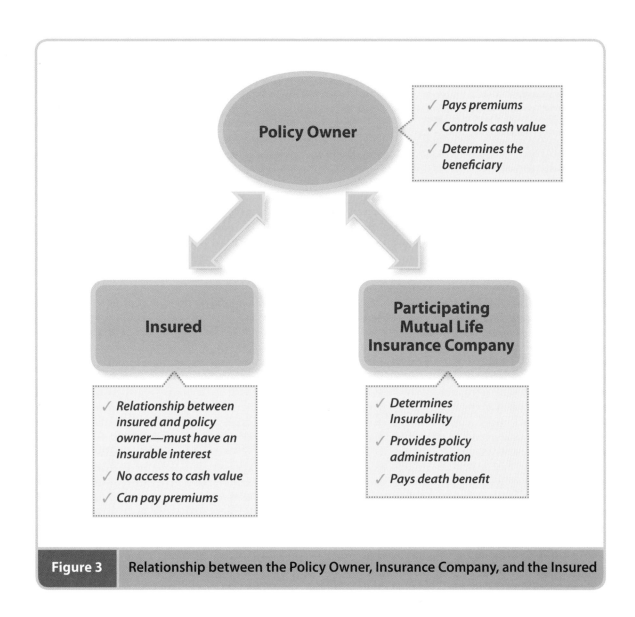

Figure 3   Relationship between the Policy Owner, Insurance Company, and the Insured

...the policy owner must have economic interest in the continued life of the insured.

including their spouse, sibling(s), child(ren), grandchild(ren), niece(s), nephew(s), or business partner(s).

To own a policy on someone else you must have an "insurable interest" in that person at the time of application for insurance. In other words, the policy owner must have economic interest in the continued life of the insured. Figure 3 illustrates the relationship between the policy owner, insurance company, and the insured.

Human life value

Another aspect of policy ownership you will hear in reference to life insurance is that of human life value. The human life value concept is used to create a basic estimate of how much insurance will be needed to cover the economic loss of the insured person.

5

Whole Life Insurance as the Cornerstone of Your Financial Strategy

A lifetime financial strategy using participating whole life insurance creates, maintains, and grows a pool of money that functions as a financial reserve you can use any way you choose. You also tap into the living benefits of participating whole life insurance allowing you to optimize the flow and movement of this money.

The living benefits of participating whole life insurance provide a financial resource for you to use and enjoy *during your lifetime*. These living benefits are present *in addition to* the legacy provided by the death benefit that will be left to your beneficiaries. Living benefits include:

- ✓ Liquidity, use, and control of your money
- ✓ Access to credit—guaranteed loans
- ✓ Flexible loan repayment
- ✓ Tax-favored environment
- ✓ Reduced loan interest, service charges, and fees paid to others

...participating whole life insurance creates, maintains, and grows a pool of money that functions as a financial reserve you can use any way you choose.

✓ No government involvement

✓ Predictable financial results

✓ Insurance for life

✓ Guaranteed insurability

✓ Guaranteed cash accumulation

✓ Creditor proof–protected asset (in certain states)

Funding a participating whole life policy from a highly rated mutual insurance company is just as easy as contributing to a 401(k)…

Funding a participating whole life policy from a highly rated mutual insurance company is just as easy as contributing to a 401(k), if not easier. The implementation is straight forward. You put the money into a whole life policy in the form of premium payments. Your money is not in the stock market. It is working for you with no risk of capital loss.

There is no need for annual balancing or realigning your asset allocation. You don't have to read financial journals or watch the stock report. Why? Because you aren't worried about what is happening with the Dow or S&P 500. Once your money is inside a whole life policy customized as a financial tool, you have access to the cash value without penalty or tax.

Your Whole Life Policy Design: The Key to Financial Performance

Not all participating whole life policies are created equal. The power and flexibility of whole life policies varies significantly among the different mutual insurance companies.

The four important elements and working parts of a participating whole life policy are: premiums, cash value, dividends, and death benefit. The way that three of these policy components (premium, cash value, and death benefit) are specifically designed to work together creates the power of using whole life as a financial tool.

A whole life policy designed as a financial tool ***must*** meet specific design criteria. Your *individual* financial requirements factor critically in designing a whole life policy that will work long-term for you and your family. It is absolutely not the case that "one size fits all."

Key Financial Benefits of Participating Whole Life

We've explored the core financial elements and characteristics to look for in a financial product that can anchor a lifetime financial strategy. When you can create a financial strategy possessing these characteristics, you will be well on your way to financial independence.

- ✓ Security and stability
- ✓ Guaranteed growth
- ✓ Access to money without penalty (financial flexibility)
- ✓ Reduced fees, service charges, and loan interest paid to others
- ✓ Tax-favored environment

Let's compare these core elements of an effective lifelong financial strategy with the strengths of a participating whole life policy designed as a financial tool.

Security and Stability

You want and need predictable financial results, without the risk of loss, to achieve financial security and stability.

A contractual guarantee within a whole life policy is that cash value grows each year as long as you pay your premiums and any

A whole life policy designed as a financial tool must meet specific design criteria.

With this type of policy, you can truly capture the power of compound interest. You therefore create a growing financial reserve that cannot experience capital loss.

outstanding loan interest. With this type of policy, you can truly capture the power of compound interest. You therefore create a growing financial reserve that cannot experience capital loss.

Guaranteed Growth

Moderate and predictable growth, combined with a 'no loss' strategy, can carry you much further than you might think. Whole life policies have guaranteed cash value and non-guaranteed dividends. The guaranteed cash value is the amount in the policy if the company were never to pay dividends.

The main point here is that with all participating whole life policies, your cash value grows as long as you pay the premiums regularly and on time. Your money is not in the stock market and your capital is not at risk.

In growing your wealth, you do not want to be limited to the amount of money you can put away or save. You will have more money some years than others to place into your financial reserve. You also need a financial vehicle that will allow you to make contributions to your financial reserve that meets your personal income, family, and tax requirements.

Your money is not in the stock market and your capital is not at risk.

In a participating whole life policy with paid-up additions, you have a built-in feature that allows increased capacity and flexibility with respect to contributions. You can contribute more money into the policy than the base premium amount. This financial flexibility is important in allowing you to make flexible contributions whenever you desire. You also have the freedom not to be locked into making high contributions if you choose to do something else with your money.

Access to Money without Penalty

Liquidity, use, and control of your money are important factors in being able to withstand a financial crisis (such as a job loss or change in health) or take advantage of an exciting investment opportunity. The cash value in your policy forms a liquid cash reserve. In the face of an unplanned life event, good or bad, you can take a loan against your policy and have immediate cash.

The cash value in your policy forms a liquid cash reserve.

Access to Guaranteed Credit

When you have a participating whole life policy, you have a built-in guaranteed credit facility. You don't need to have a job or provide pay stubs to take a loan. You do not have to qualify for this loan. The insurance company does not care about your credit score. Remember that the cash value of a whole life policy is your money. There are no fees and no need to get approved. You do not fill out mountains of loan application paperwork. Compare this process to sitting down with a loan officer at your local financial institution and what you must go through to qualify for a loan.

. . . you have a built-in guaranteed credit facility.

With a whole life policy, you also determine the timetable for when you repay your loans. You decide how often and for how long you are going to make payments. If you run into cash flow problems, you do not have to worry about making payments by a certain date each month. There are no late fees or reports sent to the credit bureaus.

As we mentioned earlier, but it's worth repeating, when you take a loan against your policy, you don't actually remove the cash value from your policy. You take a loan from the general reserves of the insurance company against your policy. The cash value in your policy actually serves as collateral for your loan. Consequently, the cash value in your policy continues to grow and receive dividends *even while you have a loan against it.*[1] This is why you have uninterrupted compounding within your policy.

You will pay interest to the insurance company on the money you borrow against your policy. But on the other hand, you are receiving dividends at the same time. This reduces your net borrowing costs considerably.

One of the best ways to control your financial life is to control who you owe your debt to, the amount of debt you have, and under what schedule you repay that debt. Participating whole life takes control out of the hands of financial institutions and credit card companies, and puts it back into yours. You can take back control of your financial life in the present and the future.

One of the best ways to control your financial life is to control who you owe your debt to, the amount of debt you have, and under what schedule you repay that debt.

Reduced Payments to Others

A whole life policy allows you to reduce the amount of loan origination fees and service charges you pay to others. By reducing loan fees and service charges, you decrease how much money you let leak out of your financial system. You get to keep more of the money you earn.

When you take a loan against your policy, you do pay interest to the insurance company. What you don't pay, however, are the additional lender service fees and loan origination fees, which can be substantial depending on the size of a loan.

Tax-Favored Environment

Whole life insurance offers a host of unique tax advantages. These can help minimize the impact of taxes on both the death benefit and cash value of your policy.

---

1. R. Nelson Nash, *Becoming your Own Banker™—The Infinite Banking Concept™*, (Birmingham, Alabama: Infinite Banking Concepts, 4th edition, 2000).

Participating whole life insurance policies enjoy favorable tax treatment. The growth of cash value is generally on a tax-deferred basis, meaning that you pay no taxes on any earnings in the policy so long as the policy remains active.

Policy loans are not considered taxable income so you can access the cash value in your policy.

Policy withdrawals up to the amount of premiums paid can be taken without being taxed.

An income tax-free death benefit ensures that your loved ones or your business receive the full value of your policy.

A Few Last Thoughts

Insurability—Something to Think About

It is possible to purchase a whole life insurance policy as an adult into your 80s *if you are insurable*. A common misconception floating around is that if you are breathing and have a heartbeat you can qualify for life insurance. Not so.

Factors such as an excessive number of motor vehicle moving violations or citations for driving under the influence (DUI) can render you uninsurable. Lifestyle choices, accidents, and illnesses may leave you unable to qualify for life insurance. Life can and does change in an instant, so remember that insurability is not guaranteed.

A common misconception floating around is that if you are breathing and have a heartbeat you can qualify for life insurance. Not so.

For Your Eyes Only—the Value of Privacy

We may not often think about our financial privacy. TransUnion®, Experian®, and Equifax® are the three major credit bureaus that report credit scores. To establish our credit-worthiness and create this score, these credit bureaus track a great deal of personal financial information along with our transaction/payment history every month.

The credit bureaus monitor such information as our address, mortgage amount and payments, our credit card balance and payment history, and any bank loans we have or have had in the past. While not exactly public information, this is a registry of many of our historical and current financial interactions. This credit information can be accessed in many ways, often disclosed in the fine print terms and conditions we have signed.

Whole Life—Privacy at no Additional Cost

Your whole life policy is a private contract between you and the insurance company.

Your whole life policy is a *private* contract between you and the insurance company. When you take a loan against your policy, no one can disclose this information but you. Your financial interactions remain private. The credit bureaus don't even know your whole life insurance contract exists.

With a whole life policy, you determine the timetable as to when to repay your loans. You decide how often and for how long you are going to make payments. There are no late fees or reports sent to the credit bureaus. Your privacy is maintained.

Financial Flexibility and Control—Who's Running the Show?

The contract you sign with the insurance company cannot be changed unless you and the insurance company both agree.

The contract you sign with the insurance company cannot be changed unless you and the insurance company *both* agree. This stands in stark contrast to the terms and conditions of credit cards. Credit card companies can and do impose changes to their usage terms.

Let's look at a common example of the one-sided terms that can be imposed by credit card companies. Suppose you are carrying an outstanding balance on your credit card. You receive a letter in the mail from your credit card company informing you that they deeply appreciate you as a customer, and also that the fixed interest rate applied to your credit card balance is changing.

After some reading of the fine print, you realize that the interest rate on your outstanding credit card balance is jumping dramatically to 16.99%. The small print at the bottom of the letter points out that if you miss one payment the interest rate on your credit card balance could increase to the maximum allowed, in some cases 29.99%.

At this point, your only option is to pay the outstanding balance on your credit card and close your account. But suppose you can't pay the balance off? Well, then you're stuck. The credit card company is in control, not you.

Remember, when you have a participating whole life policy, you have a built-in credit facility. The cash value in your whole life policy is your money. You are in control.

The cash value in your whole life policy is your money. You are in control.

6

Myths About
Whole Life Insurance

The use of whole life insurance as a financial tool tends to get short-changed, if not outright dismissed, by many financial experts. Why is this? A participating whole life policy can be a strong financial product, so why is there so much negative press out there?

This question is certainly relevant. So much so that we are going to take a whole chapter to address it. If this financial tool has ever piqued your interest, then it is important for you to understand where the critics of this approach are coming from and on what their objections are based.

Whatever financial vehicles you do choose to employ, you are responsible for understanding how they impact you and your life situation. There are strengths and limitations to any financial product. It benefits you to maximize the strengths and limit the downsides of any financial vehicle.

If you understand what might drive praise or criticism of your financial strategy, then you will not be caught by surprise or dismay if your mother-in-law, son, or the accountant you

> "Your assumptions are your windows on the world. Scrub them off every once in a while, or the light won't come in."
>
> —ISAAC ASIMOV

find yourself sitting next to on the bus voices criticism or skepticism about your approach.

When faced with a disapproving frown you smile serenely. You can acknowledge their discomfort without having to question your own financial approach. After all, *you* have done your homework. Let them do theirs.

The Conventional (or Common) View

Why don't we hear about whole life insurance as the foundation of a strong lifelong financial strategy? For starters, most of us view life insurance as an unpleasant but necessary expense. We purchase life insurance for the death benefit, so that when we die our family or other beneficiaries will be financially protected.

Although we want to protect our loved ones, it is hardly cause for celebration or excitement to focus on a product that we believe only works when we die. Purchasing life insurance can also be an uncomfortable reminder of our own mortality.

We want to buy life insurance and forget about it.

Then there is the way most insurance companies train their representatives. Think about how insurance agents approach us. Usually, they present a "financial needs analysis." This analysis determines the income, and consequently the death benefit, necessary to support dependents in the event that the main wage-earner passes away. This approach reinforces the viewpoint of life insurance as a necessary *expense*.

Often overlooked are the *powerful living benefits* of participating whole life insurance which you don't have to die to access.

Often overlooked are the powerful living benefits of participating whole life insurance which you don't have to die to access.

All Whole Life Policies are Not Created Equal

You **cannot** simply pull a participating whole life insurance policy off the shelf, dust it off, and sell it as a financial vehicle. If the premium, cash value, and death benefit of a whole life policy are not designed *specifically for use as a financial tool*, the policy will not operate optimally as a financial vehicle.

This is one of the reasons whole life insurance often gets poor reviews by the media and financial advisors. Financial experts find a whole life policy *that was never designed to work as a financial vehicle* and point out its flaws, usually by comparing it against the anticipated performance of *their* investment product(s).

It takes time, effort, and knowledge for you *and* your insurance professional to explore your financial situation. Your insurance professional cannot just complete a financial needs analysis. He or she must want to understand your personal financial situation and become familiar with your beliefs about money.

Once you've selected a qualified insurance specialist, acquiring a whole life policy for use as a financial vehicle is a two-part process: (1) you need the policy designed and structured correctly to function optimally as a financial tool, and, (2) you need your insurance specialist committed to helping and teaching you how to use it over time. Your insurance professional also needs to be committed to work with you as your financial life and needs change.

It does take time and effort to design and use a whole life policy as a financial tool. This can deter users focused on a quick return on their investment. This is a product that, as a financial tool, is meant to last a lifetime. It doesn't promise, nor does it provide, a "get rich quick" approach.

For those who are impatient, particularly for those in our modern culture seeking ever more rapid results, this strategy can seem too

It takes time, effort, and knowledge for you and your insurance professional to explore your financial situation.

Things that last take time and effort to build. And they're worth it.

slow. But we are setting up an enduring strategy, designed to work for the rest of your life.

Things that last take time and effort to build. And they're worth it.

Where's the Glamor?

If you are looking for an exciting return on your money, this strategy is not glamorous. How can you boast to colleagues at the company cocktail party that you are taking advantage of compound growth on your savings in a secure and stable financial vehicle?

It seems much more exciting to talk about the latest buzz from your broker, the potential upside of your most recent stock pick, not to mention real estate highs from days gone by.

In our opinion, if you want glamor, then buy feathers and sequins. If you want an effective financial product that enables you to build a life-long financial strategy, choose a financial vehicle that grows your money at a steady, predictable, and sustainable rate without the risk of loss.

Your Best Interest or Theirs?

You earn money. Then you pay for life necessities such as food, shelter, clothing, transportation, and education. Then, you look around at what to "do" with your remaining money. And you face an almost overwhelming array of investment and banking products.

When you invest in mutual funds within your 401(k) or in other types of investment products, Wall Street is happy. You pay brokers and fund managers to oversee your investment money. You want to see your money grow by getting a high rate of return. Along the way, though, whether your fund managers or brokers grow your money or lose it, *you* pay mutual fund fees, paper fees, service charges, and commissions on the sale of mutual funds and other investment products.

If you look to your local bank, they want to hold on to your money too. Why? Banks need your money to form their liquid reserves. Based upon these reserves, they are able to lend, grow, and prosper. Banks charge you account user fees and service charges when you place your money with them. They also make money by loaning your money back to you and charging interest and fees on each loan.

Clearly, banks and Wall Street have a self-serving interest in keeping your money under management. They exist because you pay them to hold onto, manage, and (hopefully) grow your money. They want you to turn to them with your money. Different strategies and new competitors need not apply.

It's our responsibility to use the products provided by Wall Street and banks to our advantage. We must educate ourselves as to the inherent risks and benefits of their products. We must not allow a condescending smile or a rushed personal banker to persuade us to make financial choices that are not in our best interest.

These institutions do **not** offer the only possible financial products and strategies available. There is a better way.

It's our responsibility to use the products provided by Wall Street and banks to our advantage.

The Common Approach to Life Insurance

"Buy Term and Invest the Difference"

Many financial experts we see on TV talk about getting out of debt and getting control of our finances. This is solid financial advice.

These same TV media personalities and financial "gurus" also tout the catchy but dubious advice to "buy term and invest the difference."

Table 15	Basic Whole Life Insurance vs. 20-Year Term Life Insurance for Healthy Male, Age 45		
Insurance Policy Parameters	**Basic Whole Life Insurance**	**Term Life Insurance (20-Year Term)**	
❶ Policy premium paid per year	$ 7,970	$ 980	
❷ Total policy premiums paid after 20 Years	$ 159,400	$ 19,600	
❸ Policy cash value	$ 179,920	$ 0	
❹ Death Benefit at age 65 (Year 20)	$ 537,556	$ 500,000	

So what does this phrase really mean?

We have heard and read this phrase repeatedly with respect to life insurance. But what does it mean? And what are the implications of acting on this advice without really understanding it? Let's take a look.

Table 15 is a comparison of a basic whole life insurance policy (not designed for use as a financial vehicle) compared with a 20-year term life insurance policy with a $500,000 death benefit. These life insurance policies were developed for a healthy man, age 45.

We will use the numbers in Table 15 to better understand what is meant by the phrase "buy term and invest the difference."

As you look at Table 15, you'll notice that the term life insurance premium is much lower than the whole life insurance premium (Line ❶, Table 15). The annual premium for term insurance is $980 per year and for whole life, $7,970. This is a big difference.

The premium difference between these two products is striking but so are the benefits you receive. Notice after 20 years, the term life policy owner has spent $19,600. The whole life owner has *saved* $159,400 (Line ❷, Table 15).

The difference between whole life and term insurance is that whole life policy owner still has *all* his premium payments in the policy's cash value plus an additional $20,520 in cash value (for a total of $179,920 in cash value) at the end of 20 years (Line ❸, Table 15). The whole life owner has also grown the death benefit (Line ❹, Table 15) and has had access to all the living benefits of the policy. The term life insurance owner has had life insurance coverage but no additional benefits and no forced savings.

The "buy term and invest the difference" advice the experts give attempts to make up for the fact that there is cash value accumulation in the whole life policy as compared to the term life insurance policy. The rationale goes like this:

Buy the 20-year term life insurance for $980. The difference between your annual whole life premium ($7,970) and your annual term life premium ($980) is $6,990. If you *invest* the $6,990 in the stock market for 20 years and get an 8% return every year then you will end up with $319,876 in an investment asset. This is *a lot* more ($139,956 more, to be exact) than what you accumulated in the cash value in your whole life policy over 20 years of $179,920. So by investing in the market you'll come out far ahead.

The assumption inherent in this advice is that the stock market is a great place to grow your money. That simply by putting your money in the stock market and staying there you will be fine. (Is anyone getting the least bit bored with this advice yet?).

The "buy term and invest the difference" advice does not account for the impact of variable rates of returns, capital loss, and the impact of sales commissions and fees.

Still, it would be better to invest the difference than do nothing. Often what happens is that people don't invest the difference, they *spend* the difference. So they end up with a term policy that ends at 65, no life insurance, and no investment asset.

The "buy term and invest the difference" advice does not account for the impact of variable rates of returns, capital loss, and the impact of sales commissions and fees.

y term and invest the difference" advice is also built on ption that you don't need life insurance after age 65. The oes like this: at age 65 your children or dependents will be sufficient and living on their own. Your house will be paid off. You will have enough assets and income to sustain you and your dependents for the rest of your life. No more need for life insurance.

Okay. Let's explore this line of thinking. Let's say we have a $2,000,000 death benefit in our term life insurance policy that expires on our 65th birthday. If we get hit by a truck the day *before* our 65th birthday, our spouse and family will grieve and receive $2,000,000 tax-free. Those we love will be able to use the $2,000,000 to move forward into the future, to continue with life.

If the truck hits us the day *after* our 65th birthday, our significant other and family get nothing. Yet they will suffer the same emotional loss and have the same costs and life expenses to address.

By choosing term insurance we have *deliberately* planned to reduce the assets available to our family and our estate by $2,000,000 at some pre-determined time. Does this make any sense?

Think about it. We spend a lifetime working hard, planning, and growing our wealth. We diversify our resources and use as many financial tools as possible to avoid losing money in our portfolio. We worry about the loss of our resources due to the unpredictable nature of the investment marketplace. So how does it make sense to release a $2,000,000 asset as a planned loss?

Something else to consider

Term insurance by definition is not designed for lifetime coverage. Term insurance is affordable *during* the term specified in the policy (referred to as the premium guarantee period). Often these terms are between

We spend a lifetime working hard, planning, and growing our wealth.

So how does it make sense to release a $2,000,000 asset as a planned loss?

5 and 30 years in duration. However, once the term ends, annual premiums can quickly escalate and become prohibitively expensive.

Table 16 is a typical term life insurance policy with a $2,000,000 death benefit purchased for a man, in good health, at age 35 (Line **1**, Table 16). Annual premiums within the 30-year premium guarantee period, to age 65, are $2,690 (Lines **2** and **3**, Table 16). Notice once the 30-year term is complete, should we want to continue coverage, the premium rises significantly: from a $2,690 annual premium at age 65 to $64,970 at age 66 (the 31st year the policy is in-force). As you can see from Table 16, each subsequent year after the 30-year term period (that is, after age 65), the premium escalates dramatically (Line **4**, Table 16).

So why would you want to continue term insurance past its premium guaranteed period of 30 years?

Consider the following scenario. It is not unusual.

You are approaching 65. For the past 30 years, you have paid annual premiums for your term life insurance policy with a $2,000,000 death benefit. The term ends on your 65th birthday.

One month before your birthday you are diagnosed with incurable, inoperable cancer. Your wife, also 65, has not worked outside the home in many years. Your adult son has just returned home after losing his job. He has no savings and no income. Your 401(k) has suffered significant losses. You have health insurance but your medical expenses will increase as you deal with your illness. You are deeply worried. In your absence and without your income, you don't see how your wife and son will have money to move into the future.

At this point, you look into the possibility of extending your term life insurance. The $2,000,000 tax-free death benefit would provide needed financial resources for your spouse and son. However, as Table 16 shows, with premium payments escalating from $2,690 to $64,970 over one year and continuing to grow yearly, this may not be financially feasible for you, or even in your best financial interest, regardless of the death benefit.

Table 16 — Example of a Typical 30-Year Term Life Insurance Policy (Before and After the Premium Guarantee Period)

Age of the Insured	Policy Year	Annual Policy Premium	Death Benefit
❶ 36	1	$2,690	$2,000,000
37	2	$2,690	$2,000,000
38	3	$2,690	$2,000,000
39	4	$2,690	$2,000,000
40	5	$2,690	$2,000,000
50	15	$2,690	$2,000,000
❷ 51	16	$2,690	$2,000,000
63	28	$2,690	$2,000,000
64	29	$2,690	$2,000,000
❸ 65	30	$2,690	$2,000,000
❹ 66	31	$64,970	$2,000,000
67	32	$71,170	$2,000,000
68	33	$77,650	$2,000,000
69	34	$84,490	$2,000,000

Note

The term policy continues uninterrupted from age 35 to age 65. The jagged lines in the table indicate breaks in the policy timeline for illustrative purposes only.

❶ This term life insurance policy is initiated when the owner is 35. At the end of the first year (policy year 1), the owner is 36. The annual premium and death benefit remain constant throughout the 30-year policy term (to age 65).

❷ Illustrates continued term life insurance coverage with level premium and constant death benefit.

❸ This is the last year of the premium guarantee period for the term life insurance policy (age 65).

❹ This is the 31st year of the term policy. The annual premium required to keep this policy in-force has increased from $2,690 to $64,970.

So, in this example, by choosing term insurance you have *deliberately* planned to reduce the assets available to your family and your estate by $2,000,000 at age 65.

This is the untold story many people face with the expiration of term life insurance policies. Just when you need it most, your term insurance policy may not be there.

Other Life Insurance Misconceptions

Commissions and Costs

You will often hear that insurance agents and financial advisors only sell participating whole life policies for the associated high commissions. This assumes, first, that whole life insurance is a poor product, so agents need extra incentive to promote it. And second, that agents and advisors are only in it for the money. Neither assumption is the case. Let's look at both.

A participating whole life policy, designed as a financial vehicle, is a powerful tool with strong long-term benefits.

It is true that it is not a financial product that can work for everyone. It takes a willingness to learn and act independently, and not depend entirely on your broker or the stock market. Plus, you or a close family member or relative need to be insurable. And while you don't have to be Warren Buffett, you do need a certain amount of financial capacity to fund a policy. The case studies in Chapters 8 through 13 demonstrate how this strategy can be applied to real-life scenarios.

And a word on the commissions. When an insurance professional designs a whole life policy as a financial tool, they customize it to work uniquely for you. This takes time, skill, and knowledge, and there is a commensurate cost.

Make sure you work with an insurance professional who is patient with the many questions you will have, and is able to answer

… by choosing term insurance you have deliberately planned to reduce the assets available to your family and your estate by $2,000,000 at age 65.

with clear common sense. He or she should also be committed to working with you once the policy is built and in-force. This will ensure your ability to take full advantage of its enduring stability, growth, and financial power.

You'll run into professionals in this field who choose not to perform at high standards. They overcharge, cut corners, and act indifferently to their clients' needs. They do not understand, nor are they interested in the latest developments in the industry. Don't work with these people. You don't have to. You deserve an insurance specialist dedicated to delivering the highest quality service on your behalf.

Whether you go to a doctor, plumber, or insurance specialist you want to pay for work and knowledge but not overpay. Rest assured that a reputable insurance agent with integrity will not sell you a product that doesn't work for you, just so they can make money.

And just as you'd choose your doctor, plumber, and car mechanic with a degree of care, it is wise to do the same with an insurance professional. In any industry, you will encounter a range of skill, values, and ethics. Find someone you feel comfortable with, and whose knowledge and professionalism mesh best with what you want and value.

In any industry, you will encounter a range of skill, values, and ethics. Find someone you feel comfortable with, and whose knowledge and professionalism mesh best with what you want and value.

One Size Fits All

If you were sitting in your doctor's office, and she came out and proceeded to write a prescription without so much as looking at you or asking any questions, it would be reasonable for you to run, not walk, to the nearest exit.

Don't seek or accept this treatment from financial advisors either—or from TV celebrities, columnists, or radio personalities who cannot possibly know anything about you. They are dispensing general and generic information. This *can* be useful. But understand that much of what they present is opinion, not fact.

Media personalities cannot ask questions about your particular financial situation, short- and long-term needs, nor your beliefs and values surrounding money. And, almost without exception, they promise that by staying in the stock market long-term you will come out ahead.

To achieve any true financial well-being over the long-term, please deal on a direct, personal level with financial and insurance professionals who possess knowledge and integrity. Do this whether you implement the financial approach we outline here, or consider the purchase of an investment product.

Front-Loaded Costs

You will hear people say that whole life insurance is a poor choice because it is front-loaded with costs. Yes, the costs of the actual death benefit, administration, and agent commissions are paid early in the policy. Financial experts routinely point out that the effect of this front loading is that you have to wait a long time (15 years is often quoted) before your policy's cash value equals the premiums you have paid.

This can be true of a whole life policy designed to meet insurance needs and not designed as a financial tool. A whole life policy *designed for use as a financial vehicle* will usually cover its start-up costs and begin lifelong guaranteed growth *within six or seven years.*

We are setting up a predictable, enduring, financial strategy.

Most of us are willing to make a front-loaded investment in ourselves. We readily pay the costs for education or training because we believe that we will reap the benefits of this strategy in some way for the rest of our lives.

A participating whole life policy designed as a financial tool is no different. We are setting up a predictable, enduring, financial strategy. It is going to take some time and effort to bring it to fruition. As long as we are knowledgeable about what we are doing and why we are using this approach, we can rest easy and stay the course.

… the consistent build-up of cash value within a basic whole life policy isn't necessarily a problem at all.

A Basic Whole Life Policy

The challenge with a whole life policy is to understand the difference between a basic, participating whole life policy and one that is designed and customized to be used as a financial vehicle. We'll take a close look at several customized whole life policies in our case studies in Chapters 8 through 13.

Most financial commentators and experts pull out a basic whole life policy and use this policy to explain why whole life insurance is not a good choice compared to the stock market. They show you that it takes 15 years or more to recover all the premiums and have this money available as cash value in your policy. And they are right.

However, the consistent build-up of cash value within a basic whole life policy isn't necessarily a problem at all. Your basic whole life policy is functioning exactly as it was designed to perform: to accrue savings and provide a death benefit.

Staying in the stock market long-term does not necessarily provide us protection from the depleting effect of stock market fluctuations, capital loss, and fees.

If you own a basic whole life policy, at about policy year 15, you do have an asset both with respect to the policy's cash value and the death benefit. At the 15-year mark, whether you are 40, 65, or 105, your policy does not expire. You have it for life regardless of what health issues you may face. There is great value and peace of mind in financial protection, stability, and steady growth.

The point financial commentators really want to drive home is that if you had placed your money in an investment product over 15 years rather than a basic whole life policy, you would have done much better financially.

Really? Guaranteed?

That position is built upon the projection of an average rate of return in the marketplace over 15 years.

The financial community's main assumption is that any loss you incur over these 15 years will be recovered because you will have stayed in the market over the long-term. Reality can look markedly different than these rosy estimates. Ask anyone whose 401(k) is now a 201(k).

Staying in the stock market long-term does not necessarily provide us protection from the depleting effect of stock market fluctuations, capital loss, and fees.

A Closer Look at a Basic Whole Life Policy

Let's take a look at a basic whole life policy **not** designed as a financial vehicle. The policy shown in Table 17 is a basic whole life policy for a 35-year-old man in good health. The annual premium for this policy is $20,000.

Now, if your initial reaction to this $20,000 premium is to think this is a lot of money just for insurance, hang in there. Remember, the premium payment is not an expense that buys you life insurance and then disappears. Your premium payment starts to accumulate as cash value within your whole life policy. A basic whole life insurance product is designed to function as a safe and secure **savings vehicle** while you are living. Then, this policy provides a tax-free cash payout to your family when you die.

Let's explore this policy further.

At policy year 1, age 36 (Line **1**, Table 17), there is an immediate death benefit payable of $1,928,800. However, there is little cash value available, only $731.

As we look down the column showing "Net Cash Value," we see that the cash value grows steadily each year. It is possible in *any* year to take a loan against the policy's cash value. There is no possibility of loss of the cash value from market fluctuations. The policy owner is paid a **contractually guaranteed** minimum interest rate each year. Although dividend values are not guaranteed to be paid, the policy owner is likely to receive them annually. And once a dividend is paid it becomes part of the policy's cash value.

A basic whole life insurance product is designed to function as a safe and secure savings vehicle while you are living. Then, this policy provides a tax-free cash payout to your family when you die.

Finally, the owner is not paying tax on the money growing inside his policy. Nor does the money in the policy grow into a future tax liability unless the policy is surrendered or withdrawals occur above the amount of premiums paid into the policy. This is quite different from funds in a 401(k) or other qualified plans, which will be subject to income tax upon withdrawal.

At age 50 or policy year 15 (Line ❷, Table 17), 15 years after the policy started, the owner has paid $300,000 in premiums into the policy. The policy's cash value is $305,000; the death benefit is $2,010,078. As the financial commentators have stated, which we confirm with this example, at policy year 15 the cash value within a basic whole life policy slightly exceeds the premiums paid.

Since the start of the policy, its owner has been able to access the cash value. As the policy's cash value has grown, so has the pool of money the policy owner could borrow against.

In addition, by purchasing the policy, the owner has created a future tax-free asset (i.e., the death benefit of $2,010,078) for his family or any beneficiaries he names. So the policy owner has had access to use and grow his savings while at the same time creating a future tax-free asset for his family.

After policy year 15, the cash value in the policy continues to grow. He has not lost money. Nor is he at any risk of losing money. He is not paying monthly account fees and service charges. There are no penalties should he wish to take a loan against his policy.

Should he need to finance college, a car, a business, or a vacation, he can borrow against the policy without having to justify this decision to anyone. He does not need to "qualify" for his loan, justify his credit score, fill out forms, or convince his personal banker he is worthy. The cash value within the policy is *his money*. The $305,000 cash value is available for him to borrow against. He will pay his loan back with interest, but he has the power to determine his own repayment schedule.

This is your basic whole life policy. Not really so bad. In fact, pretty good. It's not too exciting if you are looking for heady investment

Table 17 — Basic Participating Whole Life Policy on an Individual Age 35 (in Good Health)[1]

Age of Insured	Policy Year	Premium (Beginning of Year)[2]	Net Cash Value[3]	Death Benefit[3]
① 36	1	$20,000	$731	$1,928,800
37	2	$20,000	$1,523	$1,932,828
38	3	$20,000	$13,330	$1,936,963
39	4	$20,000	$32,826	$1,941,293
40	5	$20,000	$53,109	$1,945,716
41	6	$20,000	$74,202	$1,950,312
42	7	$20,000	$96,131	$1,955,244
43	8	$20,000	$118,885	$1,960,491
44	9	$20,000	$142,510	$1,966,196
45	10	$20,000	$167,021	$1,972,338
46	11	$20,000	$192,466	$1,979,039
47	12	$20,000	$218,879	$1,986,271
48	13	$20,000	$246,394	$1,993,869
49	14	$20,000	$275,103	$2,001,809
② 50	15	$20,000	$305,039	$2,010,078
51	16	$20,000	$336,279	$2,019,026
52	17	$20,000	$368,821	$2,028,799
53	18	$20,000	$402,714	$2,039,534
54	19	$20,000	$438,023	$2,051,411
55	20	$20,000	$474,803	$2,064,760
56	21	$20,000	$512,925	$2,079,227
57	22	$20,000	$552,485	$2,094,823
58	23	$20,000	$593,610	$2,111,413
59	24	$20,000	$636,380	$2,128,916
60	25	$20,000	$680,840	$2,147,445
61	26	$20,000	$727,014	$2,167,212
62	27	$20,000	$774,871	$2,188,508
63	28	$20,000	$824,452	$2,211,524
64	29	$20,000	$875,821	$2,236,319
③ 65[4]	30	$20,000	$929,055	$2,262,831

Notes

1. Hypothetical illustration that does not represent a specific product available for sale. Actual results may be more or less favorable.

2. Premiums shown are the base premium.

3. Net Cash Value and Death Benefit values listed in Table 17 assume that annual dividends have been paid.

4. The policy shown here will continue until age 121. As long as there are enough dividends earned, then the policy owner may choose the option of allowing the policy to "self-complete."

returns, but it's got some kick to it if you value steady growth and financial independence.

Take a look at this basic policy as its owner turns 65 (Line ❸, Table 17). As he gets ready to retire, he now has $929,055 in available cash value. In contrast to our term life insurance policy owner, this whole life policy will not expire at age 65.

And should his health fail, the policy owner has a death benefit of $2,262,831 to provide for his family and beneficiaries.

After the age of 65, this basic whole life policy will continue to grow until age 121 (for simplicity, we have shown the policy until age 65).

Prior to and after age 65, the policy owner also has options on how to proceed with premium payments. One option is to continue paying premiums so as to take advantage of the savings and growth capacity of the policy.

The policy owner may also choose to be able to direct the dividends paid into the policy to pay the required annual premium. As long as enough dividends are earned and/or paid-up additions are present, then the policy owner no longer needs to make premium payments to keep the policy in-force. The policy becomes "self-completing."

7

An Introduction to the Case Studies

Now we are ready to explore the power of a participating whole life policy *customized* as a financial tool. We leave behind, once and for all, the paradigm of participating whole life insurance as a necessary expense to protect our family.

The case studies presented in the next few chapters focus on specific needs and wants at different life stages and through changing life events. We subdivided these life needs, wants, and events somewhat arbitrarily by age. Remember that you can use a strategy from any of the case studies, regardless of your age, if you feel it's appropriate for you and meets your circumstances. It's truly a mix and match situation.

"Though no one can go back and make a brand new start, anyone can start from now and make a brand new ending."

—CARL BARD

Also, the various strategies and approaches provided in the case studies are meant to be illustrative, not prescriptive. We hope you will take the situations we present and adapt and use the knowledge you gain and modify it for your own specific situation.

Our main goal is to show you the financial independence that you can achieve when you get the core elements of security (no capital

You should not borrow against your policy if . . . you do not understand how this will impact your policy's performance over the long-term.

loss), growth, guaranteed access to credit, reduced fees and service charges, and a tax-favored environment all moving together in one direction.

A Few Thoughts to Keep in Mind

We have crafted these case studies to best show the strengths and diverse ways that this financial tool may be used as a cornerstone of a lifetime financial strategy. But a word of caution, a participating whole life policy is not a magic money tree. You must treat this financial tool with respect and care in order to have it to work for you over your entire life.

For example, policy loans are a very important component part of a participating whole life policy. Accordingly, in four of the case studies we show how policy loans work and how they may be used in different ways. But taking loans against the policy without regard to the policy's funding can result in the whole life policy reaching a point where no further loans are available because the maximum available loan limit has been reached. (The maximum available loan limit is a percentage of the cash value; in other words, you can't borrow a greater amount than your gross cash value).

You should not borrow against your policy if you do not believe you can pay it back in the future or you do not understand how this will impact your policy's performance over the long-term.

. . . good stewardship and responsibility are critical to the effective use of a participating whole life policy as a financial tool.

Take the time necessary to understand how your whole life policy works and the long-term impact of your choices on the policy's effectiveness. This type of information and strategy is available to you through this book and your insurance specialist.

Remember that good stewardship and responsibility are critical to the effective use of a participating whole life policy as a financial tool.

Starting your Policy

The initial policy premiums shown in the case studies vary from $5,355 per year ($465.25 per month) to $100,000 per year ($8,333.33 per month). Our primary purpose in presenting a wide range of premium amounts is to illustrate the flexibility you have with a whole life policy. A whole life policy can be started (capitalized) with money reallocated from current income, savings, qualified plans, investment income or any other income. Annual or monthly contributions to a 401(k) plan can also be redirected into a participating whole life policy on an after-tax basis.

Retirement at Age 65

We have all been trained to think of working until the age of 65 and then retiring. However, if current statistics are any indication, more and more of us may not be able to retire in the traditional sense. According to the Retirement Policy Program sponsored by the Urban Institute, researchers point out that retirement patterns are more complex and varied than in the past. They report that age 65 is "no longer a focal point for retirements."[1]

As we considered these case studies, we too recognized that 65 is an arbitrary age for retirement. It certainly doesn't seem to fit our 21st century reality so far. However, for the case studies, we needed a benchmark which reflects the point in time when you change from accumulating wealth and resources to living off your accumulated reserve and reduced income. So please keep in mind that although we use 65 as the retirement age in the case studies that follow, you can substitute any age that works for you.

1. Richard W. Johnson, Barbara A. Butrica, and Corina Mommaerts, "Work and Retirement Patterns for the G.I. Generation, Silent Generation, and Early Boomers: Thirty Years of Change." Urban Institute, The Retirement Policy Program, Discussion Paper 10-04, 2010.

Case Studies to Age 85

Participating whole life policies are built to age 121. To avoid exceedingly long tables and traumatized readers, we generally show the policy performance to age 85. It's our belief that if you can understand how the policy works to age 85, you will have the knowledge to carry you the rest of the way.

8

Case Study 1—Looking Forward at Age 35

Many of us move through our twenties without planning a great deal for our future. It feels as though we have a lot of time. Why rush?

It's natural to start thinking about our future when we commit to long-term relationships, start a family, and our career.

At this time, we think about the financial protection of those we love and who are dependent upon us. We also start looking at how to save and grow our money. In many instances, we are working for an employer who offers a 401(k) plan and perhaps a matching contribution. This becomes our first introduction into the world of qualified plans, mutual funds, and the stock market.

Our financial knowledge at this point may grow in a piece-wise fashion—a magazine article here, a TV commentator there, discussions with our work colleagues. We confuse the terms saving and investing because we haven't thought about it that much. Yet understanding

Core Elements

- ☑ Starting a Participating Whole Life Policy Customized for Financial Use

- ☑ Saving for Retirement versus Investing for Retirement

- ☑ Security and Stability

- ☑ Growth

- ☑ Financial Protection for the Family

the difference between saving and investing is critical to our long-term financial well-being.

Getting Clear at the Outset on Saving Versus Investing

As you develop a lifetime financial plan, spend time becoming clear on whether you are saving or investing. Plan for both. We run headlong into financial missteps because we do not take the time to consider what we are doing and which financial vehicles to use. A lot of retirement "savings" accounts are really retirement "investment" accounts.

To re-emphasize a point we made earlier: many financial problems arise when we use a product designed for one purpose (e.g., security and protection) but want a specific result the product is not designed to achieve (e.g., a high rate of return). We might also incorrectly expect a product primarily designed for growth, which contains a higher level of risk, to operate as a savings product.

By customizing a whole life policy to work as a financial vehicle, we can actually turbo-charge its built-in strengths.

Turbo-Charging the Power of Protection and Saving

A basic whole life policy is designed with the goals of financial protection, saving, and steady, predictable growth without the risk of loss.

By customizing a whole life policy to work as a financial vehicle, we can actually turbo-charge its built-in strengths. The core goals are to design a whole life policy that takes advantage of the living benefits much sooner, and to have greater flexibility as to the amount of money we can contribute to the policy.

By customizing the policy to act as a financial vehicle, we:

✓ Grow its cash value more quickly. This results in access to a greater percentage of our money sooner.

✓ Cause the cumulative premiums paid to equal the policy's net cash value in less than 15 years.

✓ Grow the cash value within the policy as quickly as possible, through dividends and paid-up additions, so that the cash value accumulation each year exceeds the annual premium payment.

✓ Grow tax-deferred savings.

✓ Create immediate and growing financial protection for beneficiaries.

✓ Develop a future tax-free asset: the death benefit.

✓ Ensure guaranteed access to cash without fees or penalty.

✓ Create a pool of money to supplement retirement.

The Basic Whole Life Policy versus a Policy Customized as a Financial Vehicle

A healthy 35-year-old man named Miguel and his wife, Serena, have two children. Miguel and Serena are deciding where to put their money. They are tempted to continue making contributions to Miguel's company's 401(k) plan, but it hasn't grown in the past year. Miguel's mother also needs financial assistance. Miguel and Serena are worried because they cannot access the money they have in Miguel's 401(k) should he need cash to help his mother.

Miguel and Serena investigate, and decide to implement a customized participating whole life policy (Table 18).

Table 18 — Customized Participating Whole Life Policy on an Individual Age 35 (in Good Health)[1]

	Age of Insured	Policy Year	Premium (Beginning of Year)[2]	Net Cash Value[3]	Death Benefit[3]
1	36	1	$27,015	$18,038	$1,799,066
	37	2	$27,015	$37,090	$1,895,935
	38	3	$27,015	$61,765	$1,990,759
2	39	4	$27,015	$90,729	$2,083,695
	40	5	$27,015	$121,188	$2,174,833
	41	6	$27,015	$153,195	$2,264,299
	42	7	$27,015	$186,832	$2,352,342
3	43	8	$27,015	$222,161	$2,439,063
	44	9	$27,015	$259,251	$2,524,685
	45	10	$27,015	$298,200	$2,609,375
	46	11	$26,205	$339,085	$1,793,288
	47	12	$26,205	$382,003	$1,876,510
	48	13	$26,205	$427,110	$1,958,974
	49	14	$26,205	$474,562	$2,040,686
	50	15	$26,205	$524,446	$2,121,761
	51	16	$26,205	$576,924	$2,202,515
	52	17	$26,205	$632,022	$2,283,147
	53	18	$26,205	$689,898	$2,363,907
	54	19	$26,205	$750,635	$2,445,020
	55	20	$26,205	$814,327	$2,526,875
	56	21	$26,205	$881,045	$2,609,494
	57	22	$26,205	$950,927	$2,692,960
	58	23	$26,205	$1,024,200	$2,777,237
	59	24	$26,205	$1,101,023	$2,862,299
	60	25	$26,205	$1,181,543	$2,948,334
	61	26	$26,205	$1,265,845	$3,035,715
	62	27	$26,205	$1,353,991	$3,124,864
	63	28	$26,205	$1,446,103	$3,216,134
	64	29	$26,205	$1,542,291	$3,309,689
4	65	30	$26,205	$1,642,775	$3,405,596

Age of Insured	Policy Year	Premium (Beginning of Year)[2]	Net Cash Value[3]	Death Benefit[3]
66	31	$26,205	$1,747,738	$3,503,807
67	32	$26,205	$1,857,426	$3,604,183
68	33	$26,205	$1,972,074	$3,706,775
69	34	$26,205	$2,091,973	$3,811,574
70	35	$26,205	$2,217,255	$3,918,771
71	36	$26,205	$2,348,083	$4,028,712
72	37	$26,205	$2,484,410	$4,141,969
73	38	$26,205	$2,626,318	$4,259,025
74	39	$26,205	$2,774,032	$4,379,872
75	40	$26,205	$2,927,856	$4,504,541
76	41	$26,205	$3,087,948	$4,633,164
77	42	$26,205	$3,254,488	$4,766,089
78	43	$26,205	$3,427,481	$4,903,806
79	44	$26,205	$3,606,870	$5,046,895
80	45	$26,205	$3,792,644	$5,195,764
81	46	$26,205	$3,984,837	$5,350,812
82	47	$26,205	$4,183,626	$5,512,304
83	48	$26,205	$4,389,273	$5,680,146
84	49	$26,205	$4,601,775	$5,854,562
85[4]	50	$26,205	$4,821,256	$6,036,055

Table 18 — **Customized Participating Whole Life Policy on an Individual Age 35 (in Good Health)[1] (continued)**

Notes

1. Hypothetical illustration that does not represent a specific product available for sale. Actual results may be more or less favorable.

2. Premium shown includes base premium plus paid-up additions.

3. Net Cash Value and Death Benefit values listed in Table 18 assume that annual dividends have been paid.

4. The policy shown at age 85 will continue until age 121. As long as there are enough dividends earned and/or paid-up additions, then the policy owner may choose the option of allowing the policy to "self-complete."

The money inside the policy is growing at a steady and predictable rate. There is no risk of loss. And with the death benefit, they have a future tax-free asset . . .

Miguel and Serena start the policy on Miguel when he is 35. After the first year, policy year one, Miguel and Serena have contributed $27,015 in premium (Line ❶, Table 18). The cash value available after this first year of premium is $18,038. This cash value is significantly higher than is usually available in a basic whole life policy after the first year. Recall that in the basic whole life example (Table 17), after a first-year paid premium of $20,000, the cash value was only $731.

The reason the cash value available is much higher in this case study than in the basic whole life policy in Chapter 6 is because the policy owners used paid-up additions. This allows more money to be placed in the customized policy which is then available as cash value.

The Value of a Custom-Designed Policy

Miguel and Serena now have access to two-thirds of their first year premium.

They can take a loan against the policy and assist Miguel's mother without paying withdrawal penalties and fees. Because this loan is against the policy, the money is not taxable income.

They have also protected their family with a $1,799,066 tax-free death benefit.

When Miguel turns 39 (Line ❷, Table 18), four years after the start of the policy, with each annual premium payment Miguel and Serena make, the cash value increases by more than the premium payment as a result of policy design and dividends paid into the policy. The money inside the policy is growing at a steady and predictable rate. There is no risk of loss. And with the death benefit, they have a future tax-free asset of $2,083,695 to protect their family.

Eight years after the start of the policy, Miguel is 43. The cash value in the policy is $222,161; Line ❸, Table 18. This slightly exceeds the total premiums he has paid into the policy ($216,120).

Remember that in our first look at a basic whole life policy in Chapter 6, it took 15 years for the cash value in the policy to equal or slightly exceed the premiums paid (Line **❷**, Table 17).

Miguel's custom-designed policy has reached this milestone in *eight years*—in almost half the time.

Miguel is ready to retire at age 65. This is 30 years after his whole life policy started. He does not have to worry about his life insurance policy ending at the conclusion of some pre-specified term. His whole life policy remains in-force.

Miguel and Serena have $1,642,775 available as cash value (Line **❹**, Table 18). Should he and Serena choose, they can borrow against this cash value to supplement their retirement—an amount that is not taxable because it is a policy loan. Miguel and Serena also have a $3,405,596 asset created for Serena, their children, and any other beneficiaries.

9

Case Study 2—Managing Life Events at Age 45

Allen is a single parent with one son, Michael. Allen is Senior Manager at a technology company. Michael is in his junior year in high school. College is looming. At 45, Allen wants to help fund Michael's education while continuing to save for his own retirement.

So far Allen has accumulated $430,000 in after-tax savings for his retirement. Allen knows he needs more money to retire. But leaning back in his chair, studying his account statements, Allen feels rightfully proud of his savings. He's had to overcome some tough life events to get this far.

Allen is involved with his son's educational goals and choices. He and Michael have talked about and considered college choices together. When Allen is 48, he figures he will need $30,000 per year to support Michael through four years of college.

Allen looks at this $120,000 outlay for Michael's education and shakes his head. It's a daunting amount of money. Almost one-third of his entire lifetime savings. He jokes with his

---

Core Elements

- ☑ Reallocation of Assets
- ☑ Financial Protection for the Family
- ☑ Policy Loans
- ☑ Managing Life Events:
  - Paying for College
  - Job Change
  - Retirement
- ☑ Self-Completing Policy

friends that it's like driving a new car off a cliff every year. But Allen believes Michael's education will lay a solid foundation for Michael's future. And he wants this for his son.

Starting a Policy at 45

Allen's goals are to continue to fund his retirement, support Michael's college costs, and also protect Michael financially should he (Allen) pass away unexpectedly.

Allen also wants to develop a coherent and integrated lifelong strategy that will allow him the flexibility to manage unforeseen events. Allen knows if he depletes his retirement fund to pay for Michael's college without a long-term strategy he is leaving himself in a financially weakened position. This is true with respect to his retirement fund, and also his ability to manage any unexpected life events that may come his way.

At 45, Allen has already lived through a few curve balls. He wants the financial flexibility to handle what comes his way strategically, without resorting to panicked short-term crisis management.

Allen is also tired of watching the fluctuations in his non-qualified IRA (Individual Retirement Account). He's seen his non-qualified IRA, along with his other investments, grow and shrink due to market fluctuations. At 45, Allen has had enough of this roller coaster. He wants to remove his worry factor about whether his money will be there when he needs it for his son's college education and for his retirement. He wants to be able to count on his plan to work, and for his savings to be there as he moves into his fifties and beyond.

A New Beginning

Allen decides to start a customized whole life policy as the cornerstone of his lifetime financial strategy.

Allen's insurance representative spends time with him discussing Allen's life goals, household budget, and overall financial situation. It is essential that he understand Allen's income, retirement savings, college costs for Michael, and retirement needs.

The final policy design is shown in Table 19. The premiums shown in Table 19 include base premium and paid-up additions. Let's walk through each element of this policy so we can see how Allen has prepared himself to move successfully through college planning and his retirement years.

Strong Policy Design

Reallocating Assets

Allen starts his policy when he is 45. He decides to reallocate $430,000 in after-tax savings into the policy. Allen also realizes that the money he has within his IRA is located in mutual funds, which are at risk. Allen's IRA is really an investment account and not a savings account. He wants to move his money into a vehicle that will operate as a solid savings plan with minimal risk.

Allen decides on a step-wise approach to this reallocation, moving $52,000 after-tax into his policy each year from his saving accounts. Allen also decides to redirect his after-tax investment contributions of $1,417 per month ($17,000 annually). He will redirect this $17,000 toward the policy, plus an additional $1,000 annually in savings, to reach the goal of $70,000 in premium ($52,000 plus $18,000).

Customized Participating Whole Life Policy on an Individual Age 45 (in Good Health)[1]

Age of Insured	Net Premium[2]	Annual Loan	Loan Payment	Cumulative Loan	Net Cash Value[3]	Net Death Benefit[3]
① 46	$70,000	$0	$0	$0	$52,926	$1,798,300
47	$70,000	$0	$0	$0	$108,791	$1,992,861
② 48	$70,000	$30,000	$0	$31,500	$149,821	$2,152,394
49	$70,000	$30,000	$0	$64,575	$193,859	$2,307,071
50	$70,000	$30,000	$0	$99,304	$240,187	$2,456,965
51	$40,000	$30,000	$0	$135,769	$259,170	$2,509,511
③ 52	$40,000	$0	$0	$142,557	$310,459	$2,591,008
53	$40,000	$0	$0	$149,685	$364,183	$2,671,713
54	$40,000	$0	$0	$157,170	$420,367	$2,751,762
④ 55	$40,000	$0	$15,000	$149,278	$494,788	$2,847,205
56	$30,000	$0	$15,000	$140,992	$562,718	$2,917,510
⑤ 57	$30,000	$0	$18,000	$129,142	$636,868	$2,992,231
58	$30,000	$0	$18,000	$116,699	$714,460	$3,068,388
59	$30,000	$0	$18,000	$103,634	$795,697	$3,145,992
⑥ 60	$30,000	$0	$18,000	$89,915	$880,710	$3,225,259
⑦ 61	$20,000	$0	$18,000	$75,511	$959,798	$3,284,844
62	$20,000	$0	$18,000	$60,387	$1,042,429	$3,347,322
63	$20,000	$0	$18,000	$44,506	$1,128,719	$3,413,037
64	$20,000	$0	$0	$46,731	$1,199,990	$3,463,417
⑧ 65	$20,000	$0	$0	$49,068	$1,274,523	$3,516,604
⑨ 66	$16,000	$60,000	$0	$114,521	$1,286,451	$2,903,763[4]
67	$16,000	$60,000	$0	$183,247	$1,298,443	$2,889,856
68	$16,000	$60,000	$0	$255,409	$1,310,524	$2,874,717
69	$16,000	$60,000	$0	$331,180	$1,322,727	$2,858,136
70	$16,000	$60,000	$0	$410,739	$1,334,990	$2,840,065
⑩ 71	$0	$100,000	$0	$536,276	$1,288,497	$2,750,823
72	$0	$100,000	$0	$668,090	$1,238,800	$2,658,413
73	$0	$100,000	$0	$806,494	$1,185,569	$2,562,824
74	$0	$100,000	$0	$951,819	$1,128,664	$2,463,637

Table 19

Table 19 *Customized Participating Whole Life Policy on an Individual Age 45 (in Good Health)[1] (continued)*

Age of Insured	Net Premium[2]	Annual Loan	Loan Payment	Cumulative Loan	Net Cash Value[3]	Net Death Benefit[3]
75	$0	$100,000	$0	$1,104,410	$1,067,925	$2,360,440
76	$0	$75,000	$0	$1,238,380	$1,029,176	$2,278,903
77	$0	$75,000	$0	$1,379,049	$987,171	$2,193,878
78	$0	$75,000	$0	$1,526,752	$941,507	$2,105,326
79	$0	$75,000	$0	$1,681,840	$891,761	$2,013,264
80	$0	$75,000	$0	$1,844,682	$837,502	$1,917,521
81	$0	$75,000	$0	$2,015,666	$778,315	$1,817,906
82	$0	$75,000	$0	$2,195,199	$713,904	$1,714,087
83	$0	$75,000	$0	$2,383,709	$644,001	$1,605,484
84	$0	$75,000	$0	$2,581,645	$568,104	$1,491,707
11 85[5]	$0	$75,000	$0	$2,789,477	$485,811	$1,372,559

Notes

1. Hypothetical illustration that does not represent a specific product available for sale. Actual results may be more or less favorable.

2. Premium shown includes base premium plus paid-up additions.

3. Net Cash Value and Net Death Benefit values listed in Table 19 assume that annual dividends have been paid.

4. This policy is customized to provide (1) maximum flexibility in premium contributions and (2) an increased death benefit early in the policy to ensure the greatest financial protection for Allen's son, Michael. At age 66, the death benefit adjusts as it was designed to do.

5. The policy shown here at age 85 will continue until age 121. As long as there are enough dividends earned and/or paid-up additions, then the policy owner may choose the option of allowing the policy to "self-complete."

Table 20   *Reallocating After-Tax Assets into the Policy*

Age	After-Tax Savings Contribution to Premium	Redirection of Non-Qualified IRA Annual Contribution ($17,000) and Savings ($1,000)	Premium (Sum of Both Contributions)
46	$52,000	$18,000	$70,000
47	$52,000	$18,000	$70,000
48	$52,000	$18,000	$70,000
49	$52,000	$18,000	$70,000
50	$52,000	$18,000	$70,000
Sum of Contributions Ages 46–50	$260, 000	$90,000	$350,000
51	$22,000	$18,000	$40,000
52	$22,000	$18,000	$40,000
53	$22,000	$18,000	$40,000
54	$22,000	$18,000	$40,000
55	$22,000	$18,000	$40,000
Sum of Contributions Age 51–55	$110,000	$90,000	$200,000
56	$12,000	$18,000	$30,000
57	$12,000	$18,000	$30,000
58	$12,000	$18,000	$30,000
59	$12,000	$18,000	$30,000
60	$12,000	$18,000	$30,000
Sum of Contributions Age 56–60	$60,000	$90,000	$150,000
TOTAL SUM OF ALL AFTER-TAX CONTRIBUTIONS	$430,000	$270,000	$700,000

When Allen starts his policy (Line ❶, Table 19), he pays $70,000 in premium, with a starting cash value of $52,926. He also creates a death benefit to protect his son of $1,798,300.

Table 20 summarizes Allen's planned reallocation of his after-tax money over 15 years (from the start of the policy through age 60). Remember that he has a total of $430,000 in after-tax money to re-allocate. He is also redirecting new money that he would have put into his IRA into the policy.

Allen's premium payment is designed to be flexible. He can start out making larger premium payments of $70,000 as he completes the major reallocation of his money. As the remaining funds diminish he can plan to reduce the amount of premium he pays into the policy.

The insurance term for paying the maximum premium into a policy that uses a paid-up additions rider is "overfunding." As Allen's policy demonstrates, he doesn't need to pay the maximum premium amount to keep a policy in-force. However, overfunding is a strong financial strategy because every time he puts a dollar into the policy beyond what is minimally due to keep it in-force, he increases the cash value by more than the dollar he puts in.

Paying for College

Allen has funded his whole life policy for three years (Line ❷, Table 19). His son, Michael, is ready for college, and the two of them have discussed college costs. Their agreement is that Allen is providing Michael a loan to cover his college expenses.

This is part of their joint agreement to support each other. Allen is loaning Michael money so he can afford to attend college and not worry about money while he is there. Michael has agreed to honor Allen's support and repay his dad's loan once he has finished college and has a steady income.

Allen is 48 years old when Michael's first college payment is due. Allen pays his premium of $70,000 into his policy. Allen then takes a $30,000 loan against his policy to pay Michael's college expenses.

Notice that Allen makes a very deliberate choice to put $70,000 into his policy and then take a loan against the policy of $30,000 to pay college expenses. Although he could, Allen does not reduce his premium payment to $40,000 and write two separate checks: one for his policy and one for college. Allen puts $70,000 into his policy and then takes a loan of $30,000 against the policy.

He has two specific and very good reasons for doing this: first, it takes advantage of his customized whole life policy design; and second, it captures the power of the paid-up additions built into this policy. You'll recall that paid-up additions refer to amounts of additional whole life insurance that can be added each year to a whole life insurance policy.

The Power of Paid-up Additions

Paid-up additions are fully paid-up additional amounts of insurance that increase the cash value and death benefit. A benefit of paid-up additions is that they are dividend eligible. This means the more paid-up additions you buy, the greater the potential dividend you receive annually.

By customizing the policy to allow the purchase of paid-up additions, we design a system for annual cash growth within the policy. The paid-up additions buy more death benefit and increase cash value, which in turn increase the dividends. The dividends go towards buying more paid-up additions the following year and the cycle repeats.

The real value of using paid-up additions in Allen's participating whole life policy is that Allen increases the amount of money that is going into his policy (over and above the base premium that is required to keep the policy in-force).

It Gets Better

There is another compelling reason to pay for Michael's college costs with a loan against the policy. If Allen passes away, the loans in the policy are subtracted from the death benefit. In Allen's case, if he suffered an unexpected death at age 52 (Line ❸, Table 19), the loan and loan interest of $142,557 would be subtracted from the death benefit. Michael would receive tax-free, the net death benefit shown of $2,591,008 and his college loans and interest would be paid in full.

Repayment of the College Loan

Happily though, at age 52, Allen is still in good health and enjoying life. Michael has graduated. However, the economy is slow and Michael has not been able to find a job in his field. Michael is working at a convenience store but can't afford to pay his dad back right away.

Allen and Michael have agreed once Michael lands a job in his field with longer-term potential, Michael will begin his repayment plan. Both Allen and Michael are not under pressure to start repaying college loans in a poor economy. If Michael had obtained a regular student loan, he would have struggled with the standard repayment plan requiring students to start loan payments six months after graduation.

Allen has funded his son's college education. He's also grown his retirement fund and the cash value in the policy. Allen has not worried about market fluctuations or capital loss.

As it happens, it takes Michael three years to get himself long-term employment. When Allen is 55 (Line ❹, Table 19), Michael starts repaying the loan at $1,250 per month ($15,000 per year). At this point, they have been able to let the loan sit inside the policy over three years, letting the interest accrue and be added to the loan.

Although they have accumulated interest against this loan, they have not been forced to start loan repayment until Michael was ready.

Allen and Michael have set their own loan repayment terms on their own schedule in response to an unpredictable employment market.

Allen and Michael have set their own loan repayment terms on their own schedule in response to an unpredictable employment market.

Also at age 55, Allen is approaching the last five years of his plan to reallocate his assets by age 60. He has a cumulative loan against the policy of $149,278 (Line **4**, Table 19). Despite this loan, he also has $494,788 in cash value and a $2,847,205 net death benefit.

When Allen is age 57 (Line **5**, Table 19), Michael is feeling financially able to increase his loan payments to his dad. He contributes $18,000 annually ($1,500 per month) toward repaying his loan.

Age 60—So Where is Allen Now?

At age 60, Allen has completed reallocating all his assets. He is still working and expects to redirect contributions and savings of $18,000 per year into his policy. As we can see from Table 20, Allen has reallocated and redirected a total of $700,000 into his policy.

How is Allen doing?

Looking at Line **6** (Table 19), we can see Allen is doing pretty well. He has contributed $700,000 into his policy. His policy cash value of $880,710 exceeds his total contribution of $700,000 by $180,710. And Allen has created a tax-free legacy for his son (in terms of the net death benefit) of $3,225,259.

Job Change

Allen's job situation changes as he heads into his sixty-first year. His employer, a technology company, is shifting resources. They ask Allen if he would consider working at a reduced salary. Allen's earnings drop. Even though his earnings are lower, understanding that he is in the final years of building his retirement, Allen redirects as much money as he can into his policy. This results in a premium payment of $20,000 per year ($1,666 per month); Line **7**, Table 19.

One of the chief advantages of a whole life policy is a flexible premium to accommodate life changes. Despite a decrease in income, Allen's policy is not in jeopardy. He has $959,789 in cash value should he need to borrow against the policy to finance unforeseen events.

Retirement

As Allen approaches age 65, he continues to work part-time. At age 65 he has $1,274,523 available to him in the policy's cash value (Line **8**, Table 19). The net death benefit is $3,516,604.

Allen plans to use the cash value in his policy to supplement his retirement. He will take loans against the policy and not repay them. When Allen takes a loan against the policy it creates a lien against the cash value available and reduces the death benefit. If Allen should choose to repay his loan, then the money becomes available once more as part of the cash value and death benefit.

This approach of taking loans against the policy and not repaying them has been carefully considered and planned for as part of Allen's long-term retirement strategy. This is a valid strategy as long as Allen monitors the impacts of his policy loans on his cash value and net death benefit.

Accordingly, whatever loan amount (plus interest) accumulates will be subtracted from the policy's death benefit.

The net death benefit in Allen's policy has grown and will continue to grow. Despite taking annual loans against the policy to fund his retirement, Allen's son will still receive a significant *tax-free* legacy when Allen passes away.

When Allen is 66, he contributes $16,000 per year to the policy in social security income. He also takes a loan against the policy of $60,000 to supplement his income (Line **9**, Table 19). Because Allen is taking this $60,000 as a loan against the policy, it is not subject to income tax.

Alan plans to use the cash value in his policy as his retirement fund. He will continue to take loans against the policy and not repay them.

Allen continues to benefit from paid-up additions that continue to grow the cash value and death benefit within his policy. Should Allen pass away at age 66, as sole beneficiary, Michael will receive the net death benefit of $2,903,763. Remember that the net death benefit already has the loan and loan interest amount deducted and the cash value included.

Policy Dividends Pay the Premium—You Don't

The option to allow a policy to self-complete also helps deal with unexpected life events, such as a job loss or change in health.

When Allen reaches 70, he is done with working part-time. At age 71, he takes a loan against the policy of $100,000 to supplement his retirement (Line **10**, Table 19). As a loan, this money is not subject to income tax.

Allen also chose to direct a portion of the dividends paid into the policy toward paying the required premium. This means that Allen no longer needs to make premium payments to keep the policy in-force. The policy becomes "self-completing."

At any time, in response to changing conditions, Allen can choose to reverse this option and start making premium payments again. If Allen received an inheritance, he might decide that the policy is an excellent place for this money. He could then start making premium payments again.

The option to allow a policy to self-complete also helps deal with unexpected life events, such as a job loss or change in health. Choosing the self-complete option for even a year or two before resuming premium payments can reduce financial pressure, keep the policy in-force, and allow financial flexibility simply unavailable in other financial products.

Allen is happy. At 71 and into the future, he has elected not to make premium payments. His loans against the policy are tax-free income. He does not have to worry about market fluctuations decimating his retirement.

Table 19 shows Allen taking loans against the policy until age 85—loans he does not have to repay. If we look at the policy status when Allen is age 85 (Line **11**, Table 19), the net death benefit available to Michael is $1,372,559.

This net death benefit of $1,372,559 is the amount of money Michael will receive tax-free if his father passes away at age 85. The loans and loan interest are already subtracted from the death benefit to arrive at the 'net death benefit' shown in Table 19.

10

Case Study 3—Planning for the Future at Age 55

Jane, 55, has established her own business buying homes, renovating them, and reselling them. She has two grown children living in different cities pursuing their own lives and careers.

Jane's husband passed away unexpectedly a few years ago. At times, Jane finds herself feeling anxious about relying solely on herself and her business to fund her retirement. And, she wants to leave a legacy for her children. At some point in the next 10 years, Jane would also like to stop work and take time to visit her friends, travel, and spend time with her children.

When Jane looks at her investment accounts, she feels uneasy. Her retirement investment accounts are not doing that well. All but one investment fund has lost money over the last year.

> **Core Elements**
> ☑ Reallocation of Assets
> ☑ Build and Grow Savings
> ☑ Business Loans
> ☑ Optimize Social Security Payments
> ☑ Assist Aging Parents
> ☑ Inheritance
> ☑ Retirement Income

She looks ahead to the next 10 years and knows she needs to ensure her money will be there for retirement. She cannot afford any more losses. She dreads the next call from her broker which starts with the words, "Sorry, Jane."

Jane is also tired of dealing with banks. Each time she applies for a business loan to renovate a house she needs to provide an ever-growing mountain of documentation. She thinks that with her track record and high credit rating, the loan process would get easier. But it never does.

There's always a new business loan officer to deal with, plus different forms and requirements. The inevitable hoops include three years of business financial records, personal guarantees, statements of assets, and personal net worth, etc. It makes Jane want to reach for a dry martini. And Jane doesn't drink.

After much thought and a fair bit of research, Jane decides to start a customized participating whole life policy. She's looking for growth, stability, and flexibility. She also wants access to credit for her business without continually having to prove she's worthy.

Table 21 is the policy Jane has implemented at age 55. Let's walk through Jane's policy and explore how it meets her short- and long-term goals.

Reallocating Assets with a Custom-Built Strategy

Jane first decides to reallocate the $500,000 after-tax investment balance into her policy in annual increments. The first policy year, Jane pays $100,000 (after-tax) in premium into her policy (Line ❶, Table 21).

Jane does not have to place $100,000 worth of premium to get her policy started. In Jane's case, the minimum premium required to keep the policy in-force is $22,702 (which decreases to $22,000 at age 68).

In consultation with her insurance specialist, Jane adopts a specific strategy where she 'overfunds' the policy by paying the maximum amount of premium allowed. Using this approach, the death benefit provided by the policy grows more quickly. Every dollar Jane puts into the policy beyond what is minimally due to keep it in-force results in an increase in the death benefit by more than the dollar she added.

Business Loans Without Red Tape

When Jane is 58, she has owned the policy for three years (Line ❷, Table 21). She has now reallocated assets of $300,000. During this third year, Jane needs capital to finance a home renovation. She takes a loan against her policy of $150,000.

Jane couldn't be more delighted with the loan process. She doesn't need to provide any financial statements, fill out confusing forms, prepare a statement of net worth, provide three years of business financials, or answer calls from the loan officer questioning her statements and business transactions.

All Jane did to take a loan against her policy was to fill in a loan request form and submit it to her insurance company. On this form, she provided her name, policy number, and loan amount. That's it. There were no loan origination charges, no service fees, no initial finance charges, no closing fees, no commissions, and no hassles.

She can't quite believe the process is this simple. She questions her insurance agent, John. Surely she is missing something? John confirms that since Jane is borrowing against the cash value within her policy, her check for $150,000 will simply show up in the mail in about a week or so.

John explains that Jane's loan against the policy creates a lien against the cash value and death benefit in the policy. If Jane pays back her loan and interest, then the principal payments made will become available once more as part of the cash value and death benefit. If she chooses not to repay the loan, then this $150,000 loan amount (plus interest) will be subtracted from the death benefit. It's that simple. Jane gets to choose what she wants to do.

There were no loan origination charges, no service fees, no initial finance charges, no closing fees, no commissions, and no hassles.

Table 21 — Customized Participating Whole Life Policy on an Individual Age 55 (in Good Health)[1]

	Age of Insured	Net Premium[2]	Annual Loan	Loan Payment	Cumulative Loan	Net Cash Value[3]	Net Death Benefit[3]
❶	56	$100,000	$0	$0	$0	$77,927	$1,831,253
	57	$100,000	$0	$0	$0	$160,082	$2,059,373
❷	58	$100,000	$150,000	$0	$157,500	$106,974	$2,127,241
❸	59	$100,000	$0	$85,000	$76,125	$297,917	$2,431,636
❹	60	$100,000	$0	$76,125	$0	$488,810	$2,728,704
❺	61	$22,702	$300,000	$0	$315,000	$217,632	$2,440,332
	62	$22,702	$0	$180,000	$141,750	$436,470	$2,641,222
❻	63	$22,702	$0	$141,750	$0	$625,657	$2,811,608
	64	$22,702	$350,000	$0	$367,500	$307,519	$2,473,722
	65	$22,702	$0	$0	$385,875	$340,513	$2,486,025
❼	66	$100,000	$0	$385,875	$0	$857,695	$2,471,821
❽	67	$100,000	$450,000	$0	$472,500	$522,665	$2,198,963
	68	$22,000	$0	$200,000	$286,125	$775,850	$2,428,218
	69	$22,000	$0	$200,000	$90,431	$1,041,147	$2,668,461
	70	$22,000	$0	$90,431	$0	$1,204,060	$2,805,172
❾	71	$22,000	$150,000	$0	$157,500	$1,122,146	$2,696,118
	72	$22,000	$150,000	$0	$322,875	$1,035,537	$2,581,542
	73	$22,000	$150,000	$0	$496,519	$944,002	$2,461,166
	74	$22,000	$150,000	$0	$678,845	$847,341	$2,334,838
	75	$22,000	$150,000	$0	$870,287	$745,328	$2,202,360
❿	76	$22,000	$0[4]	$500,000	$388,801	$1,319,741	$2,745,210

Table 21 — *Customized Participating Whole Life Policy on an Individual Age 55 (in Good Health)[1] (continued)*

Age of Insured	Net Premium[2]	Annual Loan	Loan Payment	Cumulative Loan	Net Cash Value[3]	Net Death Benefit[3]
77	$22,000	$150,000	$0	$565,741	$1,239,395	$2,632,178
78	$22,000	$150,000	$0	$751,528	$1,153,973	$2,512,961
79	$22,000	$150,000	$0	$946,605	$1,063,186	$2,387,135
80	$22,000	$150,000	$0	$1,151,435	$966,673	$2,254,333
81	$22,000	$80,000	$0	$1,293,007	$937,320	$2,188,203
82	$22,000	$80,000	$0	$1,441,657	$904,476	$2,119,062
83	$22,000	$80,000	$0	$1,597,740	$867,966	$2,046,566
84	$22,000	$80,000	$0	$1,761,627	$827,670	$1,970,263
11 85[5]	$22,000	$80,000	$0	$1,933,709	$783,211	$1,890,002

Notes

1. Hypothetical illustration that does not represent a specific product available for sale. Actual results may be more or less favorable.

2. Premium shown includes base premium plus paid-up additions.

3. Net Cash Value and Net Death Benefit values listed in Table 21 assume that annual dividends have been paid.

4. Instead of taking a $150,000 loan against the policy this year, Jane decides to keep $150,000 from her $650,000 inheritance and place the rest ($500,000) into her policy.

5. The policy shown here at age 85 will continue until age 121. As long as there are enough dividends earned and/or paid-up additions, then the policy owner may choose the option of allowing the policy to "self-complete."

John also confirms that Jane is in total control of her loan repayment schedule. No one will be calling or sending form letters to her outlining her loan repayment terms or fixed repayment schedule.

Jane is delighted. She takes the $150,000 and uses it to renovate and upgrade her latest home. For the first year of her loan, she makes no loan payment (Line **2**, Table 21). In the next two years, as Jane turns 59 and then 60, Jane decides to repay her loan (Lines ❸ and ❹, Table 21).

As Jane repays her loan within these two years, she continues to reallocate her assets and overfund her policy by paying $100,000 in premium.

By age 60 (Line ❹, Table 21), five years after Jane started her customized participating whole life policy, Jane has repaid her $150,000 loan and completed the reallocation of her investment assets. She has $488,810 in cash value, slightly under the $500,000 she has paid into the policy in premiums. During this time, she has also been able to take advantage of the built-in guaranteed credit facility within the policy for her business.

At age 61 (Line ❺, Table 21), Jane reduces her premium payment to $22,702. She has expanded her business and is completing two home renovations. She takes a loan against the policy of $300,000. To best manage her business cash flow, Jane decides not to pay loan interest or make any loan payments the first year. Over the next two years, she sells her homes and repays her loan such that she is able to optimize her business cash flow.

Growing her Money and her Legacy

By the time Jane is 63 (Line ❻, Table 21), just eight years after the policy was initiated, she has $625,657 in cash value. Jane has paid $568,106 into the policy. Her policy cash value now exceeds the amount she has paid in premiums by $57,551. Jane has effectively used the policy to take loans of $450,000 to operate and manage her business expenses without needing to qualify for business loans through her bank. Should Jane pass away unexpectedly, she has created a legacy of $2,811,608 (net death benefit) for her children.

With all her business activities and stress, Jane has been able to watch her money grow steadily and without concern. She no longer fears calls from her broker with news her investments have dropped in value but not to worry. Jane has been able to focus on her business and her family without wondering what will happen to her money in the future. A great relief!

Helping Aging Parents

When Jane is 64, her father falls ill and passes away. Her mother has medical bills, limited assets, and failing health. Jane needs to assist her mother financially. Jane takes a loan against the policy of $350,000. She uses this money to help her mother cope financially with the transitions she must make: dealing with increased health care costs, selling the family home, moving, finding, and paying for long-term care.

It is a stressful time for Jane and her mother. There is much heartache. However, since Jane is able to help her mother financially, this eases the stress her mother is experiencing.

It takes eight months to sell her mother's home. Even longer to see the finances finalized and her mother settled. Jane makes no loan payments for two years. When she is 66, she is able to repay the principal plus interest on the policy loan with funds from the sale of her parent's home.

Leveraging a Final Business Loan

At 66, Jane's business is going well. As she nears retirement in the next few years, Jane decides she wants to put as much as she can into her policy. At 66 and 67 she makes premium payments of $100,000 each year (Lines **7** and **8**, Table 21).

When Jane is 67 (Line **8**, Table 21), she takes her largest loan against the policy yet ($450,000). She is completing several renovations and this is her last big series of projects before she retires.

Notice that Jane makes an educated decision to contribute $100,000 into her policy as premium and then take a loan against the policy of $450,000. She chooses this first strategy rather than pay less premium and take a smaller loan. Why?

By putting $100,000 of premium into the policy and then taking a loan against the policy of $450,000, Jane is taking advantage of her customized whole life policy design and the paid-up additions built into her policy.

By deliberately paying the maximum premium she can, and then taking a loan (rather than decreasing her premium payment), Jane uses the paid-up additions to increase the amount of money going into her policy.

When Jane overfunds the policy in this way, she uses the paid-up additions rider to purchase additional whole life insurance. The payment of dividends on the paid-up additions causes the additional amount of money inside Jane's policy (specifically the death benefit and cash value) to compound. This growth is an important cornerstone of a participating whole life policy designed as a financial vehicle.

Social Security and the Whole Life Policy

At 68, Jane starts to draw her Social Security. She uses her Social Security income of $12,000 and $10,000 of income to fund the policy. She also uses her business reserves to repay her $450,000 loan.

In her seventy-first year, Jane decides to retire. She continues to use her Social Security combined with her personal income to fund the policy. However, at 71, Jane also starts to take a loan against the policy of $150,000 per year to supplement her retirement (Line **9**, Table 21). Because Jane is taking this $150,000 as a loan against the policy, it is not subject to income tax.

Jane plans to use the cash value in her policy as her retirement fund. She will continue to take loans against the policy and not repay them.

With a solid income and free time, Jane travels, visiting her children and her mother. She is enjoying her freedom and her life. She is not worried about money or stock market volatility or her investment portfolio.

Receiving an Inheritance

Sad news. When Jane is 76 her mother passes away. Jane receives a tax-free inheritance of $650,000 via her mother's life insurance policy. Usually, it's challenging to know what to do with a large lump sum of money. However, Jane has no such concerns.

Jane decides not to take a loan of $150,000 against her policy this year. Instead she keeps $150,000 of her inheritance and puts the remaining $500,000 into her whole life policy (Line **10**, Table 21). By placing this money in the policy, she repays part of the loan she made against the policy and this increases her cash value and death benefit. Her cash value within the policy climbs to $1,319,741 and her death benefit reaches $2,745,210.

Jane is not dependent upon her children for support. She is able to continue to take annual loans against the policy of $150,000 to fund her retirement.

Jane's Unique Policy Design

Jane continues to flow her Social Security ($12,000) and other income ($10,000) into the policy to make her premium payments. If she wanted, Jane could also opt not to make any premium payments and have the policy "self-complete." However, in Jane's situation, this is not necessary.

By flowing her Social Security and personal income through the policy and not opting for the policy to "self-complete," Jane accomplishes the following:

- ✓ She creates additional growth in her policy which far exceeds her contribution.

- ✓ Her entire income remains liquid should she need or want it.

- ✓ She grows the death benefit for her children.

Leaving a Legacy

Jane was fortunate to receive an inheritance from her mother's life insurance policy.

Similarly, Jane wants to create a financial legacy for her children. Her children are not expecting it. They don't even want to talk about it. But it makes Jane feel happy and satisfied knowing that she can help them in this way.

Jane's policy is set to continue to age 121. She can continue her retirement strategy using her Social Security income to assist making her premium payments and taking loans against the policy as long as she lives.

Table 21 shows Jane's policy until age 85 (Line **11**, Table 21). If Jane passes away at 85, she will leave her children a tax-free inheritance of slightly under $2 million ($1,890,002).

Jane is at peace with her choices and her financial decisions. Regardless of how long she lives, she has created a future free of financial worry.

11

Case Study 4—Looking Forward to Retirement at Age 63

Saul has worked all his life as an electrical engineer. He'd be the first to tell you he has weathered some ups and downs in life starting with his first wife and ending with his second. But as Saul moves into his early sixties, he has managed to accumulate $600,000 after-tax.

Saul has done pretty well to accumulate his $600,000 after-tax reserve. An inheritance plus investments, the stock market and otherwise, helped. But he decided it was time to get out of the market, and now Saul's money rests in his savings account. Saul doesn't want to risk it in the market but he doesn't know what to do with it.

The more Saul investigates difference financial products, the more he decides that he wants to establish a retirement vehicle for himself that provides the best tax advantages. He knows that he will need his entire $600,000 to fund his retirement. Saul also realizes that unless he changes his strategy he won't be able to leave much of an inheritance to his daughter and son.

Core Elements

- ☑ Reallocation of Assets
- ☑ Build and Grow Savings
- ☑ Eliminating Market Risk
- ☑ Optimizing Social Security Payments
- ☑ Retirement Income
- ☑ Providing a Legacy

Table 22 — Customized Participating Whole Life Policy on an Individual Age 63 (in Good Health)[1]

	Age of Insured	Net Premium[2]	Annual Loan	Loan Payment	Cumulative Loan	Net Cash Value[3]	Net Death Benefit[3]
❶	64	$100,000	$0	$0	$0	$87,440	$1,450,633
	65	$100,000	$0	$0	$0	$179,598	$1,649,278
	66	$100,000	$0	$0	$0	$282,578	$1,846,227
	67	$100,000	$0	$0	$0	$390,620	$2,041,752
	68	$100,000	$0	$0	$0	$503,914	$2,236,150
❷	69	$100,000	$0	$0	$0	$622,706	$2,429,758
❸	70	$12,268	$50,000	$0	$52,500	$608,087	$2,403,930
	71	$12,268	$50,000	$0	$107,625	$592,430	$2,376,444
	72	$12,268	$50,000	$0	$165,506	$575,632	$2,347,232
	73	$12,268	$50,000	$0	$226,282	$557,626	$2,316,221
❹	74	$7,798	$50,000	$0	$290,096	$538,329	$1,283,321
	75	$7,798	$50,000	$0	$357,100	$517,654	$1,248,449
	76	$7,798	$50,000	$0	$427,455	$495,486	$1,211,475
	77	$7,798	$50,000	$0	$501,328	$471,750	$1,172,305
	78	$7,798	$50,000	$0	$578,895	$446,318	$1,130,820
	79	$7,798	$50,000	$0	$660,339	$419,147	$1,086,933
	80	$7,798	$50,000	$0	$745,856	$390,114	$1,040,520
	81	$7,798	$50,000	$0	$835,649	$358,951	$991,695
	82	$7,798	$50,000	$0	$929,932	$325,335	$940,633
	83	$7,798	$50,000	$0	$1,028,928	$289,161	$887,152
	84	$7,798	$50,000	$0	$1,132,875	$250,183	$830,776
❺	85[4]	$7,798	$50,000	$0	$1,242,018	$208,146	$771,372

Notes

1. Hypothetical illustration that does not represent a specific product available for sale. Actual results may be more or less favorable.

2. Premium shown includes base premium plus paid-up additions.

3. Net Cash Value and Net Death Benefit values listed in Table 22 assume that annual dividends have been paid.

4. The policy shown here at age 85 will continue until age 121. As long as there are enough dividends earned and/or paid-up additions, then the policy owner may choose the option of allowing the policy to "self-complete."

At 63 Saul is in reasonable health. He sees his friends' health changing and knows life circumstances can turn quickly. He has had term policies before but the last term policy ended when he was 60.

Saul decides not to gamble with his insurability and starts to look into purchasing a participating whole life policy.

Saul is careful about choosing an insurance representative who is knowledgeable about using whole life as a financial tool. One of the questions Saul uses to evaluate the various agents he talks with is whether they use a participating whole life policy themselves. Saul also wants to be clear that his insurance professional is using his or her own policy as a financial vehicle.

Saul meets and chats with insurance professionals until he is comfortable he has found a good fit based upon industry knowledge, references, values, and his own comfort level. Saul and his new insurance specialist, Sarah, meet to discuss Saul's financial situation, along with Saul's goals, and his values and beliefs about money. Sarah designs and customizes Saul's whole life policy to yield the maximum cash value as a financial vehicle.

At 63, feeling confident in this path and his chosen insurance specialist, Saul purchases his first participating whole life insurance policy.

After one year, at age 64 (Line **1**, Table 22), Saul has contributed $100,000 into his policy. After this first year, Saul has $87,440 available as cash value. He also has a $1,450,633 legacy (the net death benefit) for his children.

Building Wealth Tax-Free

Over the next six years, Saul continues to reposition his assets. He moves $100,000 per year into his whole life policy. By age 69 (Line **2**, Table 22), six years after he started the policy, his cash value ($622,706) exceeds the premium of $600,000 he has paid into the policy. Saul also has a death benefit of $2,429,758 available tax-free to his beneficiaries (in this case, his children).

At 70 (Line ❸, Table 22), Saul starts to receive Social Security income of $12,268 per year. He uses his Social Security income to continue to fund the policy. At the same time, Saul also starts to take an annual loan against the policy of $50,000 to supplement his retirement. Since Saul is taking this $50,000 as a loan against the policy, it is not subject to income tax nor does it show up as earned income on his annual income tax return.

Saul plans to use the cash value in his policy to supplement his retirement. He will continue to take loans against the policy and not repay them. This strategy of taking loans against the policy and not repaying them has been carefully considered and planned in consultation with Saul's insurance specialist, Sarah. Sarah has informed Saul that this is a valid strategy as long as Saul monitors the impact of his policy loans on his cash value and net death benefit.

So when Saul considered his long-term approach involving policy loans, he carefully reviewed the impact of this approach on his whole life policy with Sarah. Saul and Sarah monitor how Saul's policy loans are impacting the policy to make sure the policy is operating efficiently and is funded appropriately to keep it in-force now and in the future.

A Less Certain Future

What if Saul had stayed with conventional advice and put as much money as he could in his 401(k) plan (or any qualified plan)?

Two issues would have emerged as Saul considered his long-term retirement options. First, Saul would not be able to predict how much money he would have in his 401(k) in the future. He could guess, he could hope, but he would not have a solid number on which to plan.

Because Saul could not predict how much money he would have had in his qualified plan, he also would be unable predict what tax

This strategy of taking loans against the policy and not repaying them has been carefully considered and planned . . .

bracket he would be in and consequently, what his tax rate would be when it came time to take disbursements from his 401(k).

The bottom line: with mutual funds in a 401(k) plan as Saul's sole retirement strategy (other than Social Security income), Saul would not be able to quantitatively manage his retirement income or his tax liability throughout his retirement years with any certainty. Sure, he could make some estimates, but these numbers would be all subject to change, depending upon market conditions.

Conventional wisdom also says that Saul's tax bracket will decrease in retirement. Perhaps. But no one has a crystal ball. What if the tax rates increase? Saul has no control over what tax regulations and rules will be in effect at the time he would want to withdraw his money from his 401(k). It's comforting to hear financial experts make the claim that Saul's tax bill will be lower in retirement but, quite frankly, this is simply a guess.

This is the challenge of qualified plans.

This is the challenge of qualified plans. The money goes into a 401(k) or 403(b) or other qualified plan Saul might have had before-tax, but his tax bill does not get forgiven. His tax bill simply waits patiently and accumulates right along with any money he makes. Or worse, his tax bill is still there even if he loses money inside his 401(k). For example, suppose Saul had started with a $100,000 balance in his 401(k) and his 401(k) mutual fund balance dropped to $40,000. Even though the balance in his 401(k) decreased, he would still have a tax liability on the $40,000 within his 401(k) upon its disbursement.

His tax bill simply waits patiently and accumulates right along with any money he makes.

A More Certain Future

With his participating whole life insurance policy, Saul places money into the policy after-tax. He has already paid his tax bill and consequently life is a lot simpler. Also, money that grows inside Saul's policy is not taxable income. This is because dividends paid are considered a return of premium, and are not taxed while in the policy.

Saul is not worried that the $50,000 that he borrows against his whole life policy will increase his tax rate because it's a loan against the policy, and not taxable income.

Saul also understands the terms of his policy with the insurance company. It is a private contract. This means that unlike qualified plans that are subject to government jurisdiction and changing rules, the insurance company cannot change the rules (or terms) of the policy without Saul agreeing to them.

With a solid tax-free $50,000 per year, free time, and no worries about money, Saul starts dating again. He's enjoying life.

At 74 (Line ❹, Table 22), Saul decreases the policy premium payments he makes into the policy from $12,268 to $7,798.

... he will leave a legacy of $771,372 for his children— more than his entire life savings of $600,000.

He does this because he can. He has flexibility with respect to his premium payment. Should he so choose, Saul can also decide to modify the operating parameters of the policy so that any dividends paid to the policy will be directed toward reducing his policy loans. This thereby offsets the total cost of his $290,096 loan.

Saul has flowed $742,648 into his policy and has taken loans against the policy of $800,000 (i.e., a $50,000 loan each year for 16 years). At age 85 (Line ❺, Table 22), he will leave a legacy of $771,372 for his children—more than his entire life savings of $600,000.

12

Case Study 5—The Power of Guaranteed Access to Credit—At Any Age

Many policy owners do not realize what a potent credit facility they have within their whole life policy. This case study focuses on the strength of using your whole life policy and its built-in access to guaranteed credit.

But wait, you say, haven't we covered this already? Haven't we already talked about taking loans against the policy to pay for college, assist aging parents, and supplement retirement income?

Yes, but here's the bottom line. We have not yet explored the tremendous financial *power and benefit* of using the loan capability of your whole life policy to fund large *routine* purchases over your lifetime. (Large routine purchases can be defined as those that cannot be paid for out of your monthly cash flow).

This may seem minor to you compared with paying for college and retirement. But stay with us here. Funding large routine capital purchases, such as a car, with a loan against your policy, instead of paying cash or taking a bank loan, offers the following advantages:

> ### Core Elements
>
> ☑ The Power of Guaranteed Access to Credit
>
> ☑ Eliminate Payment of Fees and Service Charges to Financial Institutions
>
> ☑ Build and Grow Savings
>
> ☑ Create Your Own Financial System

✓ enhanced growth and access to the cash value within your policy

✓ creation and growth of a separate asset (the death benefit)

✓ no need to qualify for a loan

✓ a secure savings program

✓ ability to set your own loan repayment schedule

✓ elimination of fees and service charges paid to others

✓ transaction privacy

✓ no universal default clauses or unilateral loan provisions

✓ immediate clear title to your car (no bank lien)

We don't realize how much financial freedom we can achieve by using the credit capability that is built-in and available to us as whole life policy owners.

Conventional Purchasing

How do most of us make large routine capital purchases? Usually, we go about this in two main ways: (1) we take a loan from a bank or other lender and pay this loan back; or (2) we save and pay cash up front.

Don Blanton has devised a series of graphs (Figures 4 and 5) illustrating this conventional thinking.[1]

The Debtor

Many of us fall into this category. We need to purchase a car, so we head to our bank or lender and go through the process of qualifying

---

1. Don Blanton, *Circle of Wealth® System*, by Money *Trax*, Inc., "Debtor, Saver, Wealth Creator Visual," *The Private Reserve Strategy*™, January 2012.

for a loan. If we fill out all the paperwork, if our credit score is acceptable to the lender, if we can get through the application process and qualify for the loan, the financial institution will lend us money to buy our car.

We can only use this loan to buy a car. The lending institution sets forth the terms for loan interest, loan origination fees, and repayment—including our monthly loan repayment amount and schedule. If we fail to meet these terms, our lender repossesses the car. The lender can do this because when we obtain a car loan they place a lien against the vehicle title to ensure that they get paid for the outstanding loan. If you sell your car or truck, the lien against the title ensures that your car loan is paid in full to your lender before you receive any money.

This is the scenario many of us find ourselves in because we need a car but must access credit to pay for one. This is the common way we have been taught to buy a car.

Using this approach, our car purchase process looks something like the graph below.

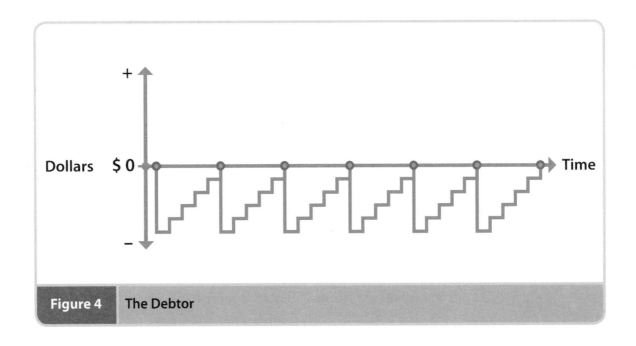

Figure 4   The Debtor

At the beginning of the process we owe nothing. So we start at zero. We take a loan to finance our purchase, then pay it back in incremental steps to get back to our zero starting position. Along the way, we pay loan interest and fees to our lender. We are happy when we get back to zero. Often, though, there is a short time period before we need a new vehicle or other major purchase and we start this cycle again.

The Saver

You might think that the Saver is in a better place. Admittedly, no loan interest accrues because the Saver has the money for the purchase up front. Also, as the Saver puts money away, there may be some interest and tax liability accumulating on the money being saved. However, to maintain liquidity, the Saver may not place his or her money in a financial product designed for growth.

Consequently, the Saver's car purchase process looks like this:

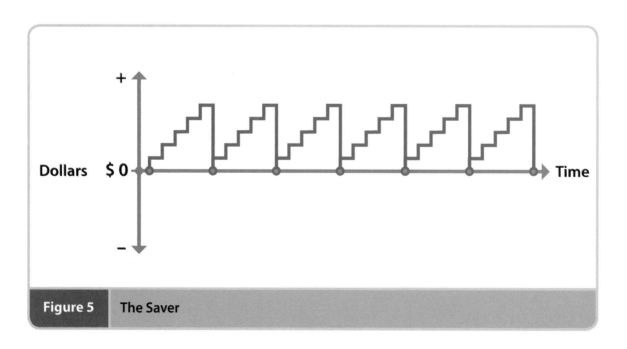

| Figure 5 | The Saver |

The Saver starts at zero and saves incrementally. Once enough money is accumulated, then he or she spends it and purchases the car. By spending all the money, the Saver is back at a zero position. He or she then starts the incremental savings process again in anticipation of the next major capital purchase.

Again, a common approach to purchases and one with which we are all familiar.

And neither the Debtor nor the Saver comes out ahead on these major capital purchases.

There is another way.

The Wealth Creator[2]

This is where the power of using the built-in credit capability of a custom-designed participating whole life policy comes into its own.

The credit facility within a whole life policy is guaranteed. So there is no loan application or qualifying process. How can this be? Because when you borrow from the insurance company and take a loan against your policy, you do not actually withdraw money from your policy. You take a loan using the financial reserves of the insurance company. Your policy cash value and death benefit act as collateral for the loan.

If you pay back your principal and loan interest, then the principal becomes available once more as part of the cash value and death benefit inside your policy. If you choose not to repay the loan, then when the insured person dies, the outstanding loan balance (plus interest) is subtracted from the death benefit.

Since you have a private contract with the insurance company, your loan transaction remains private. The credit bureaus are not involved.

And neither the Debtor nor the Saver comes out ahead on these major capital purchases. There is another way.

2. Don Blanton, *Circle of Wealth® System*, by Money *Trax*, Inc., "Debtor, Saver, Wealth Creator Visual," *The Private Reserve Strategy*™, January 2012.

Growing Your Wealth over Time

Take a look at the graph below. The Wealth Creator starts with a custom-designed participating whole life policy. The dotted green line reflects the growth of the cash value within the policy. After the policy is initiated, the policy owner decides to take a loan against the policy (shown by the solid green line) and buy a car. As with any

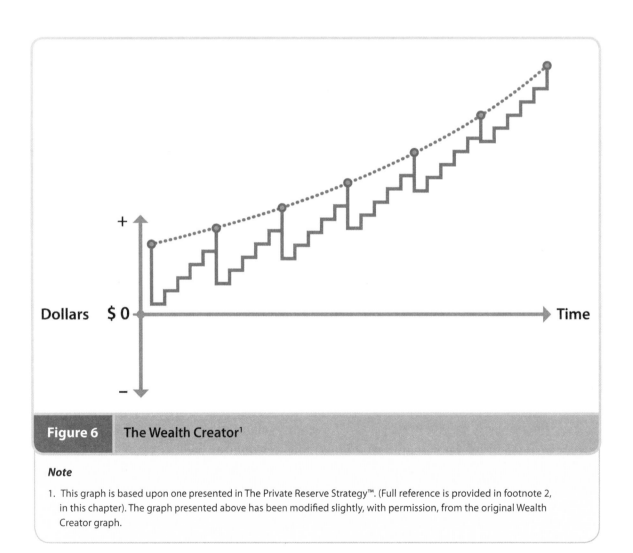

Figure 6	The Wealth Creator[1]

Note

1. This graph is based upon one presented in The Private Reserve Strategy™. (Full reference is provided in footnote 2, in this chapter). The graph presented above has been modified slightly, with permission, from the original Wealth Creator graph.

loan, the policy owner pays back this loan incrementally in a step-wise fashion. But unlike a loan from a bank, there is no qualifying process, no loan origination fees, no service charges, and no rigid loan repayment schedule.

The policy owner pays loan principal and interest back to the insurance company. With each payment, the insurance company incrementally releases the lien against the policy. The power of the participating whole life contract is that the money in your policy continues to compound and grow while you have a loan against it. Your repayment of the policy loan and interest reduces the lien, restoring your access to capital and maximizing the death benefit.

The policy owner borrows money to fund capital expenses, save money, and grow an additional asset (the death benefit) at the same time. In a custom-designed whole life policy, which uses paid-up additions to strategic advantage, taking loans from the insurance company against the policy and paying them back causes a multiplier effect and grows the cash value and the death benefit.

Over time, the policy owner takes loans, makes capital purchases, repays the loans with interest, **but does not end up back at zero at the conclusion of each purchase cycle.** Wealth grows throughout the policy owner's lifetime.

With this *Wealth Creator* graphic in mind, let's take a look at our case study.

Using Your Policy to Buy a Car

Naomi and Ichiro are turning 30. Ichiro is a realtor. He spends a lot of time in his car with clients. It's important to Ichiro that his car reflects the professionalism he brings to his work. Naomi is a graphic designer and commutes 20 miles each way to work. She wants to drive a vehicle with a strong safety and performance record.

The power of the participating whole life contract is that the money in your policy continues to compound and grow while you have a loan against it.

As Naomi and Ichiro navigate building their careers, they discuss their long-term life and financial goals with their insurance specialist. They haven't decided whether to start a family. But they do want to be smart about how they make, use, and manage their money.

Their insurance professional, Denise, suggests they investigate participating whole life insurance as a turbo-charged savings strategy. Denise also points out that with proper policy design, Naomi and Ichiro will be able to use the built-in credit facility to make large capital purchases such as cars.

Ichiro is hesitant about a participating whole life policy. As a real estate professional he has experienced wide swings in his income. The thought of being tied to an annual premium payment when his income is variable makes Ichiro nervous.

Denise understands Ichiro's concerns. She discusses Ichiro and Naomi's household income, their conservative anticipated cash flow, and their need for reliable cars. After several consultations, Denise designs a policy to meet Ichiro and Naomi's unique financial situation. Due to Ichiro's good health, Ichiro and Naomi decide to purchase a participating whole life policy on Ichiro.

The final policy design is shown in Table 23. A core component in the custom-designed policy Denise has created is the use of premium and paid-up additions. Let's walk through each component of this policy so we can see how Denise has designed the policy to work for Naomi and Ichiro.

Initial Premium Payments

Ichiro and Naomi are worried about their changing and unpredictable income. To address this concern, their insurance professional designed their whole life policy with Ichiro and Naomi contributing $40,000 in total premium payments over four years. These premium payments include both the base premium and paid-up additions. They have this money available to them partly as savings, via their investments, and through their decision to contribute to the policy annually from their future income.

At the start of their custom-designed policy (Line **1**, Table 23), Ichiro and Naomi pay $10,000 in premium annually. The first year, due to the power of paid-up additions, this $10,000 premium payment generates $8,338 in cash value *and* creates an additional asset of $415,839 (the net death benefit).

In the first year of their policy Ichiro and Naomi also have access to over 80% of their first year premium payment (as cash value).

Naomi and Ichiro continue to make annual premium payments of $10,000 for four years. In their fourth year, when Ichiro is 34, they have contributed a total of $40,000 in premium payments into their policy (Line **2**, Table 23). At this time, they have a cash value of $37,540 and a death benefit of $573,828.

In the four years since they started the policy, Ichiro and Naomi have had a baby girl, Akira. If Ichiro should pass away unexpectedly, Naomi has $573,828 to help her live and cover her family's expenses. Naomi will have the funds to allow her time to grieve and find a way forward without financial panic.

Fortunately, at 35, Ichiro is the picture of health. His real estate career is blossoming. Ichiro and Naomi decide it is time to purchase a new car for Ichiro.

Ichiro and Naomi take a $25,000 loan to purchase a new car (Line **3**, Table 23). They decide on a loan repayment schedule of $600 per month ($7,200 per year).

Due to Ichiro and Naomi's concerns regarding cash flow, Denise customized the policy so that separate premium payments were not necessary after the initial contribution of $40,000 into the policy. Denise accomplished this by strategic policy design. The policy design allows for a single annual loan repayment. The annual loan repayment incorporates repaying the car loan plus interest, along with additional savings, which together, also pay for the premium.

Table 23 Customized Participating Whole Life Policy on an Individual Age 30 (in Good Health)[1]

	Age of Insured	Net Premium[2]	Annual Loan	Loan Payment[3]	Cumulative Loan	Net Cash Value[4]	Net Death Benefit[4]
❶	31	$10,000	$0	$0	$0	$8,338	$415,839
	32	$10,000	$0	$0	$0	$17,098	$469,926
	33	$10,000	$0	$0	$0	$26,647	$522,571
❷	34	$10,000	$0	$0	$0	$37,540	$573,828
❸	35	$0	$25,000	$7,200	$26,250	$19,864	$581,123
	36	$0	$0	$7,200	$20,160	$31,846	$602,875
	37	$0	$0	$7,200	$13,765	$44,422	$624,624
	38	$0	$0	$7,200	$7,050	$57,615	$646,387
❹	39	$0	$0	$7,200	$0	$71,624	$469,086
	40	$0	$30,000	$8,400	$31,500	$51,712	$473,119
	41	$0	$0	$8,400	$24,192	$67,691	$499,446
	42	$0	$0	$8,400	$16,518	$84,448	$525,846
	43	$0	$0	$8,400	$8,460	$102,022	$552,375
	44	$0	$0	$8,400	$0	$120,437	$579,101
	45	$0	$35,000	$9,600	$36,750	$98,769	$578,573
	46	$0	$0	$9,600	$28,224	$119,228	$608,260
	47	$0	$0	$9,600	$19,271	$140,670	$638,177
	48	$0	$0	$9,600	$9,870	$163,163	$668,335
	49	$0	$0	$9,600	$0	$186,767	$698,724
	50	$0	$40,000	$10,800	$42,000	$164,204	$693,357
	51	$0	$0	$10,800	$32,256	$190,083	$725,959
	52	$0	$0	$10,800	$22,024	$217,192	$758,903
	53	$0	$0	$10,800	$11,281	$245,593	$792,277
	54	$0	$0	$10,800	$0	$275,322	$826,160
	55	$0	$45,000	$12,000	$47,250	$252,739	$816,239
	56	$0	$0	$12,000	$36,288	$284,848	$852,278
	57	$0	$0	$12,000	$24,777	$318,424	$888,976
	58	$0	$0	$12,000	$12,691	$353,553	$926,330
	59	$0	$0	$12,000	$0	$390,305	$964,359
	60	$0	$50,000	$13,200	$52,500	$368,727	$950,600
	61	$0	$0	$13,200	$40,320	$408,174	$990,462

Table 23 — Customized Participating Whole Life Policy on an Individual Age 30 (in Good Health)[1] (continued)

Age of Insured	Net Premium[2]	Annual Loan	Loan Payment[3]	Cumulative Loan	Net Cash Value[4]	Net Death Benefit[4]
62	$0	$0	$13,200	$27,530	$449,353	$1,031,270
63	$0	$0	$13,200	$14,101	$492,307	$1,073,142
⑤ 64	$0	$0	$13,200	$0	$537,097	$1,116,179
⑥ 65	$0	$30,000	$0	$31,500	$529,506	$1,098,421
66	$0	$30,000	$0	$64,575	$521,253	$1,079,787
67	$0	$30,000	$0	$99,304	$512,316	$1,060,126
68	$0	$30,000	$0	$135,769	$502,644	$1,039,326
69	$0	$30,000	$0	$174,058	$492,218	$1,017,273
70	$0	$30,000	$0	$214,260	$480,958	$993,911
71	$0	$30,000	$0	$256,473	$468,795	$969,238
72	$0	$30,000	$0	$300,797	$455,584	$943,278
73	$0	$30,000	$0	$347,337	$441,204	$916,027
74	$0	$30,000	$0	$396,204	$425,590	$887,344
75	$0	$30,000	$0	$447,514	$408,692	$857,100
76	$0	$30,000	$0	$501,390	$390,397	$825,164
77	$0	$30,000	$0	$557,959	$370,594	$791,479
78	$0	$30,000	$0	$617,357	$349,124	$756,008
79	$0	$30,000	$0	$679,725	$325,810	$718,750
80	$0	$30,000	$0	$745,211	$300,460	$679,612
81	$0	$30,000	$0	$813,972	$272,906	$638,516
82	$0	$30,000	$0	$886,170	$243,011	$595,326
83	$0	$30,000	$0	$961,979	$210,641	$549,806
84	$0	$30,000	$0	$1,041,578	$175,595	$501,811
⑦ 85[5]	$0	$30,000	$0	$1,125,157	$137,680	$451,221

Notes

1. Hypothetical illustration that does not represent a specific product available for sale. Actual results may be more or less favorable.

2. Premium shown includes base premium plus paid-up additions.

3. Loan payments have been designed to include loan, loan interest, premium, and paid-up additions.

4. Net Cash Value and Net Death Benefit values listed in Table 23 assume that annual dividends have been paid.

5. The policy shown here at age 85 will continue until age 121. As long as there are enough dividends earned and/or paid-up additions, then the policy owner may choose the option of allowing the policy to "self-complete."

Take a look at Line **4**, Table 23. At this time, Ichiro and Naomi have finished paying for their car. They have paid $7,200 per year ($600 per month) over five years. This has amounted to $36,000 in payments into the policy. The original loan was $25,000. The $11,000 difference between the car loan and their payments have paid the policy premium, car loan, loan interest, and have contributed to their policy's cash value. At this point in time, Ichiro and Naomi also have a net cash value in their policy of $71,624.

This policy design also includes having any dividends declared by the insurance company directed toward purchasing paid-up additions.

By using the policy to make a large capital purchase, such as a car, they have paid loan interest to the insurance company as they would to a bank. However, in using their whole life policy as a credit facility, they have avoided the hassle involved in qualifying for a loan, loan origination fees and service charges, and a structured repayment schedule. In addition, they have complete flexibility as to how and when they repay their loan.

Another Benefit of a Policy Loan

Over the next 25 years, Ichiro and Naomi continue to use their policy to buy cars. With each loan, Ichiro and Naomi set up their own repayment schedule and pay the loan principal and interest back to the insurance company. As these loan payments are received, the insurance company incrementally releases the lien against the cash value and death benefit. This results in a growing policy cash value with each loan repayment. This increasing cash value is then available for other purchases and life events.

The process of incrementally releasing the lien against the cash value and death benefit as loan payments are received (and causing the cash value to increase) *stands in stark contrast* to traditional loans from financial institutions.

The lien the bank or other lender places against a car is *not released until the entire car loan has been fully repaid.* Suppose Ichiro and Naomi had obtained a standard car loan from a bank and had defaulted on one of their final loan payments. Regardless of how close to paying off their loan they are, due to their default, the lender would be within their rights to repossess the car.

The Power of Savings

Naomi and Ichiro have benefited from using the built-in credit facility available within their whole life policy. They have used policy loans to fund new cars throughout their life together.

When Ichiro is 64 (Line ⑤, Table 23), Ichiro and Naomi have $537,097 in cash value. They have a net death benefit of $1,116,179. All they have done with the policy is used its credit capability to buy new cars. Of course, they have also been responsible in setting up loan repayments and establishing a repayment schedule that has worked to fit their household income and cash flow.

Ichiro and Naomi have used the credit facility in their whole life policy to fund major capital purchases (in their case, new cars). During this time, their participating whole life policy has also functioned as a simple and powerful secure savings program. The cash value within their policy has grown by more than the loan repayment amounts, including the loan interest paid.

Compare the available cash value when Ichiro is 64, $537,097 (Line ⑤, Table 23), to their total policy contributions of $346,000 (Line ①, Table 24).

Table **24**	**Total Direct Policy Contributions**[1]	
Initial Premium Payments (including premium and paid-up additions)		$40,000
Sum of All Policy Contributions[1]		$306,000
① Total Direct Contributions to the Policy		$346,000

Note

1. Policy contributions consist of the loan repayment, loan interest, premium, and paid-up additions.

Moving Into the Future

Let's take a final look at Ichiro and Naomi as they retire. Ichiro is gearing down his real estate practice. When he is 65, he and Naomi decide to use the credit facility of Ichiro's policy in a different way.

Now Ichiro and Naomi will take a $30,000 loan against the policy to fund their cars and supplement their travel and other retirement expenses. Since Ichiro and Naomi are taking this $30,000 as a loan against the policy, it is not subject to income tax (Line ⑥, Table 23).

Ichiro and Naomi plan to continue to take loans against the policy to supplement their retirement fund. In fact, they take annual loans of $30,000 against the policy until Ichiro reaches 85 (Line ⑦, Table 23). At this time, they have taken $630,000 in loans against the policy ($30,000 per year times 21 years).

So when Ichiro and Naomi considered this long-term approach involving policy loans, they carefully reviewed the impact of this approach on Ichiro's whole life policy with their insurance specialist. Ichiro and Naomi monitor their policy to ensure that the policy is operating efficiently and is funded appropriately to keep it in-force now and in the future.

At 85, using their policy, Ichiro and Naomi have created $630,000 in tax-free income over 21 years. With a death benefit of $451,221 (Line **7**, Table 23), they are leaving more to their daughter, Akira, than the total amount of direct contributions into the policy $346,000, (Line **1**, Table 24).

Getting Everything Working For You

As Ichiro and Naomi glide off into the sunset, it's worth taking a moment to summarize what they accomplished with their whole life policy.

By taking advantage of a thoughtful and customized policy design that met their specific needs and life situation, Ichiro and Naomi were able to get all the components of their financial system working together and in sync.

Consider that the only real direct purpose Ichiro and Naomi had for their whole life policy was to purchase cars. However, because they were responsible and paid back their loans and because their policy was properly designed for their life situation, they benefited from:

- ✓ Guaranteed access to credit—when they needed to access money for a car loan, it was easy. No need to fill out loan application paperwork, no worry about credit scores, income confirmation, etc.
- ✓ Reduced loan origination fees and service charges to others.
- ✓ Flexibility—policy design that incorporated base premium and paid-up additions allowing access to cash value and growth of this cash value.

✓ Security and stability—no capital loss.

✓ Growth—the cash value and death benefit have grown through payment of paid-up additions and repayment of loan and loan interest. Additional growth within the policy has also occurred as a result of dividend payments.

✓ Tax benefits—loans against the policy are not considered taxable income. Although they contribute to the policy with after-tax dollars, the growth of the money inside the policy is not taxed.

✓ Legacy—they have created a financial legacy for Naomi and Akira, while enjoying the living benefits of the policy while Ichiro is alive.

When you have a solid foundation, you can build something that lasts.

Naomi and Ichiro's whole life policy became a cornerstone of their lifetime financial plan. Regardless of what other investment products or vehicles they might have, they have been able to count on their participating whole life policy to provide the benefits listed above.

When you have a solid foundation, you can build something that lasts. This is what Ichiro and Naomi have accomplished.

13

Case Study 6—a Multi-Generational Strategy

The core strengths of participating whole life insurance as the foundation of a lifetime financial strategy are 1) the prevention of capital loss, 2) the compounding of money uninterrupted over time, and 3) establishing the liquidity, use and control of your money without restrictions.

Obtaining a whole life insurance policy on ourselves or anyone in whom we have an insurable interest, such as our child, grandchild, niece, or nephew (and remaining the policy owner), can open up the power of this financial tool.

... this is an excellent wealth-building strategy.

Many insurance critics will caution that a whole life insurance policy on a child is a waste of money. Remember, we establish a participating whole life insurance policy on a child not because he or she needs insurance to protect any dependents, but because this is an excellent wealth-building strategy. We are looking at whole life insurance as a financial tool.

As we move through our late twenties and early thirties, we tend to get more serious about saving money. If we anticipate retiring at 65, and we start saving at 30, this gives us 35 years to take advantage of the power of compound growth.

By starting a policy on a child who is five, we capture the power of compounding over a time span of *60 years*. During this time, our money inside the whole life policy experiences no capital loss, no drainage from fees, and it grows through the power of compound growth. As with any participating whole life policy, all the living benefits are available including use of the policy's cash value to fund life events.

A whole life policy on a child allows you to capture time and make it work for you.

A whole life policy on a child allows you to capture time and make it work for you.

Planning for the Future

You set up a participating whole life policy on a child to develop a multi-generational financial strategy. Parents and children then work together to fund and use the living benefits and the death benefit of participating whole life insurance to create a financial legacy that can span family generations.

Parents may initially set up the policy directly, or with loans they take against the cash value in their own whole life policies.

Preparing to handle changing life circumstances by being in control of your money is a solid multi-generational financial strategy.

As the child's policy grows, the child's parents may opt to take a loan against the cash value in their child's policy to fund or supplement their retirement. When one of the parents passes away, the outstanding loan (with interest) in the child's policy can be repaid by the death benefit from the parent's policy. Death benefits are income tax-free.

Using the living benefits of whole life allows the policy owners to capture the power of compound interest, reduce the impact of capital loss, and manage payments of loan interest and fees to others.

Who knows what the future will bring? Preparing to handle changing life circumstances by being in control of your money is a solid multi-generational financial strategy.

Grandparents Start a Child's Policy

Mai-li and Chang have a son, Huan, who is turning five. They have spent time thinking about their lifelong financial strategy. Chang is self-employed and owns his environmental consulting practice. Mai-li is a lawyer.

Mai-li and Chang are familiar with the financial strengths of participating whole life insurance. They have whole life insurance policies in place for each of them. Their whole life policies form the foundation of their lifelong financial plan.

Chang's grandparents have approached Chang and Mai-li. As a way to share their wealth and provide a lifelong gift to Huan, they want to start a whole life policy on Huan, their only grandchild.

In the process of obtaining their whole life policies, Mai-li and Chang know that, for the protection of children, most insurance companies also have underwriting guidelines other than health which must be met before an insurance policy will be issued on a child. These requirements vary between insurance companies but include such considerations as the amount of insurance coverage on parents, and/ or grandparents. However, since Mai-li and Chang have their own whole life policies, Huan's grandparents will be able to start a policy on their grandson.

Huan's grandparents review their finances and meet with their insurance professional. Huan's grandparents decide to contribute $446.25 per month or $5,355 in premium annually into Huan's policy. Huan's grandparents will maintain ownership of the policy, not Mai-li and Chang.

The policy is designed such that premium payments include base premium and paid-up additions. When Huan is six (Line ❶, Table 25), Huan's grandparents have contributed $5,355 in premium and the available cash value is $3,356.

Table 25 — Customized Participating Whole Life Policy on a Child Age 5 (in Good Health)[1]

Age of Insured	Net Premium[2]	Annual Loan	Loan Payment	Cumulative Loan	Net Cash Value[3]	Net Death Benefit[3]
❶ 6	$5,355	$0	$0	$0	$3,356	$555,505
7	$5,355	$0	$0	$0	$6,896	$609,501
8	$5,355	$0	$0	$0	$10,632	$662,076
9	$5,355	$0	$0	$0	$14,577	$713,264
❷ 10	$5,355	$0	$0	$0	$19,186	$763,141
11	$5,355	$0	$0	$0	$25,174	$811,734
12	$5,355	$0	$0	$0	$31,451	$859,176
13	$5,355	$0	$0	$0	$38,006	$905,497
14	$5,355	$0	$0	$0	$44,851	$950,764
15	$5,355	$0	$0	$0	$51,954	$995,159
16	$5,355	$0	$0	$0	$59,289	$1,038,719
17	$5,355	$0	$0	$0	$66,883	$1,081,533
18	$5,355	$0	$0	$0	$74,760	$1,123,672
19	$5,355	$0	$0	$0	$82,982	$1,165,189
20	$5,355	$0	$0	$0	$91,598	$1,206,113
❸ 21	$5,355	$0	$0	$0	$100,621	$1,246,396
22	$5,355	$0	$0	$0	$110,116	$1,286,115
23	$5,355	$0	$0	$0	$120,095	$1,325,346
24	$5,355	$0	$0	$0	$130,574	$1,364,028
25	$5,355	$0	$0	$0	$141,575	$1,402,237
26	$5,355	$0	$0	$0	$153,120	$1,439,984
27	$5,355	$0	$0	$0	$165,224	$1,477,277
28	$5,355	$0	$0	$0	$177,909	$1,514,124
29	$5,355	$0	$0	$0	$191,305	$1,550,600
30	$5,355	$0	$0	$0	$205,417	$1,586,627
31	$5,355	$0	$0	$0	$220,303	$1,622,268
32	$5,355	$0	$0	$0	$236,015	$1,657,589
33	$5,355	$0	$0	$0	$252,554	$1,692,582
34	$5,355	$0	$0	$0	$269,964	$1,727,245

Table 25 — Customized Participating Whole Life Policy on a Child Age 5 (in Good Health)[1] (continued)

Age of Insured	Net Premium[2]	Annual Loan	Loan Payment	Cumulative Loan	Net Cash Value[3]	Net Death Benefit[3]
34	$5,355	$0	$0	$0	$269,964	$1,727,245
35	$5,355	$0	$0	$0	$288,277	$1,761,642
36	$5,355	$0	$0	$0	$307,532	$1,795,771
37	$5,355	$0	$0	$0	$327,710	$1,829,631
38	$5,355	$0	$0	$0	$348,880	$1,863,288
39	$5,355	$0	$0	$0	$371,064	$1,896,808
40	$5,355	$0	$0	$0	$394,334	$1,930,187
41	$5,355	$0	$0	$0	$418,681	$1,963,423
42	$5,355	$0	$0	$0	$444,130	$1,996,579
43	$5,355	$0	$0	$0	$470,720	$2,029,655
44	$5,355	$0	$0	$0	$498,446	$2,062,712
45	$5,355	$0	$0	$0	$527,339	$2,095,811
46	$5,355	$0	$0	$0	$557,442	$2,128,892
47	$5,355	$0	$0	$0	$588,827	$2,162,012
48	$5,355	$0	$0	$0	$621,628	$2,195,222
49	$5,355	$0	$0	$0	$656,008	$2,228,453
50	$5,355	$0	$0	$0	$691,999	$2,261,748
51	$5,355	$0	$0	$0	$729,595	$2,295,151
52	$5,355	$0	$0	$0	$768,776	$2,328,653
53	$5,355	$0	$0	$0	$809,502	$2,362,302
54	$5,355	$0	$0	$0	$851,787	$2,396,160
55	$5,355	$0	$0	$0	$895,601	$2,430,291
56	$5,355	$0	$0	$0	$940,897	$2,464,695
57	$5,355	$0	$0	$0	$987,751	$2,499,433
58	$5,355	$0	$0	$0	$1,036,352	$2,534,524
59	$5,355	$0	$0	$0	$1,086,856	$2,569,969
60	$5,355	$0	$0	$0	$1,139,281	$2,605,839
61	$5,355	$0	$0	$0	$1,193,440	$2,642,119
62	$5,355	$0	$0	$0	$1,249,178	$2,678,814

Table 25 — Customized Participating Whole Life Policy on a Child Age 5 (in Good Health)[1] (continued)

Age of Insured	Net Premium[2]	Annual Loan	Loan Payment	Cumulative Loan	Net Cash Value[3]	Net Death Benefit[3]
63	$5,355	$0	$0	$0	$1,306,411	$2,715,986
64	$5,355	$0	$0	$0	$1,365,097	$2,753,624
65	$5,355	$0	$0	$0	$1,425,342	$2,791,756
66	$5,355	$0	$0	$0	$1,487,221	$2,830,378
67	$5,355	$0	$0	$0	$1,550,904	$2,869,495
68	$5,355	$0	$0	$0	$1,616,542	$2,909,096
69	$5,355	$0	$0	$0	$1,684,242	$2,949,191
70	$5,355	$0	$0	$0	$1,754,001	$2,989,778
71	$5,355	$0	$0	$0	$1,825,752	$3,030,903
72	$5,355	$0	$0	$0	$1,899,171	$3,072,616
73	$5,355	$0	$0	$0	$1,974,016	$3,114,990
74	$5,355	$0	$0	$0	$2,050,391	$3,158,001
75	$5,355	$0	$0	$0	$2,128,386	$3,201,657
76	$5,355	$0	$0	$0	$2,207,998	$3,245,973
77	$5,355	$0	$0	$0	$2,289,137	$3,291,013
78	$5,355	$0	$0	$0	$2,371,428	$3,336,802
79	$5,355	$0	$0	$0	$2,454,567	$3,383,381
80	$5,355	$0	$0	$0	$2,538,325	$3,430,786
81	$5,355	$0	$0	$0	$2,622,500	$3,479,059
82	$5,355	$0	$0	$0	$2,707,035	$3,528,205
83	$5,355	$0	$0	$0	$2,792,043	$3,578,226
84	$5,355	$0	$0	$0	$2,877,461	$3,629,126
85[4]	$5,355	$0	$0	$0	$2,963,031	$3,680,905

Notes

1. Hypothetical illustration that does not represent a specific product available for sale. Actual results may be more or less favorable.

2. Premium shown includes base premium plus paid-up additions.

3. Net Cash Value and Net Death Benefit values listed in Table 25 assume that annual dividends have been paid.

4. The policy shown here at age 85 will continue until age 121. As long as there are enough dividends earned and/or paid-up additions, then the policy owner may choose the option of allowing the policy to "self-complete."

Huan's grandparents continue to contribute to the policy. By the time Huan is 10 (Line ❷, Table 25), the cash value is $19,186. When Huan turns 21 (Line ❸, Table 25), the cash value in the policy is $100,621. Huan's grandparents have contributed $85,680 in premium toward the policy. They have not had to worry about loss of their money. It has been growing in a safe and secure vehicle.

Consider that, at age 21, should his grandparents so choose, they can transfer ownership of the policy to Huan. Or, they can continue to maintain policy ownership, but use the living benefits within the policy to help Huan learn about strong financial stewardship. Huan's grandparents can use the policy's living benefits to help Huan purchase a car and to support Huan in his college education.

By starting a policy on Huan, his grandparents have captured the power of time and compound growth. This policy allows the opportunity for a multi-generational, wealth-building strategy that will help finance Huan's life needs.

Huan's grandparents have given him a gift of love and support that will last a lifetime.

14

Moving Forward

As we wrap up we believe that it's worth taking inspiration from the fitness expert Jack LaLanne. A self-described emotional and physical wreck while growing up in the San Francisco area, Mr. LaLanne began turning his life around after hearing a talk on proper diet at age 15.

He started working out with weights when they were an oddity. In 1936 he opened the prototype for the fitness spas to come—a gym, juice bar, and health-food store—in an old office building in Oakland, California.

Doctors, however, advised their patients to stay away from his health club, a business totally unheard of at the time, and warned their patients that "LaLanne was an exercise 'nut' whose programs would make them muscle-bound and cause severe medical problems."[1]

It's amazing to look back now and consider how the prevailing experts were wrong about the effects of exercise and fitness. It's worth considering that many of the financial experts focused on the late 20th century financial paradigm may not be right either.

---

1. Richard Goldstein, "Jack LaLanne, nutrition and fitness guru, dies at 96," *The New York Times*, January 23, 2011.

… we're not going to create financial strategies for ourselves that are flexible, responsive to change, and work in both a strong and weak economy, by doing what we've always done.

"Stay in the stock market, ride out the down-turn, the market will rebound"

"Invest for the long-term"

"Focus on your rate of return"

Given the new paradigm facing us in the 21st century, we're not going to create financial strategies for ourselves that are flexible, responsive to change, and work in both a strong and weak economy, by doing what we've always done. And just like Mr. LaLanne, perhaps we need to challenge the status quo and step outside the box of conventional thinking.

The key to moving through and responding to change is to seek new knowledge and be open to new ideas.

Looking to the 21st Century with Confidence

We live in challenging times. But we can choose how to face our future. As we move into the 21st century, we can think back to those who faced the start of the 20th century.

Our early 20th century forefathers saw huge scientific, cultural, political, and technological changes. Think about the impact of the light bulb, the automobile, airplanes, radio, television, antibiotics, frozen food, world wars, birth control, nuclear arms proliferation, terrorism, climate change, and computers. Oh yes, and as our daughter would be quick to point out, the cell phone and texting.

Our ancestors, whether by force of personality or sheer lack of other available resources, depended on their own counsel, ability, and self-wisdom. They believed they were smart enough to handle their present and future.

We are too. We need to seek knowledge and education. But we also need to rely on our own intelligence. We can decide what is right for us, financially, or in any other way.

By slowly taking control of those things that are truly within our control, such as our finances, we can gain a measure of peace of mind and security. Who knows what the 21ˢᵗ century will bring? Being prepared to handle changing life events and circumstances by understanding our financial situation and being in control of our money is the cornerstone of a solid life plan. At any age.

Resolve to make your financial choices with knowledge and a clear sense of your own financial direction. By taking charge and choosing guaranteed, predictable financial growth without unnecessary losses, you can grow and enjoy your wealth efficiently for your entire life.

Consider that the goal is to build a financial strategy that will truly last a lifetime. Once we develop our skill and our financial knowledge, then we are in a position to thoughtfully choose the appropriate financial products that fit into and support this strategy.

Participating whole life insurance customized and used as a financial tool can form the cornerstone of your financial strategy in the 21ˢᵗ century. The foundation of this strategy is built on predictable results, financial control, and lifetime access to your cash without penalty.

No matter where we want to go, we must begin our journey from where we are. As the Chinese philosopher Lao-tzu so appropriately stated, *"The journey of a 1,000 miles begins with a single step."* Begin now. An exciting future awaits.

Resolve to make your financial choices with knowledge and a clear sense of your own financial direction.

15

Choosing Your Insurance Specialist

This book has touched upon the importance of finding and selecting the right insurance specialist for you. You want to consider both the qualifications of the insurance representative and the financial strength of the insurance company.

Almost anyone licensed to sell life insurance can obtain a participating whole insurance policy for you. However, since a participating whole life policy becomes the cornerstone of your lifetime financial strategy, you want to ensure it is properly customized to fit you.

The insurance representative you select must understand your personal financial situation and be familiar with your values and beliefs about money.

As you speak to agents, to find one who's right for you, ask them these questions:

✓ Do they have a participating whole life policy themselves?

✓ Do they have participating whole life policies on their children?

✓ Do they use their whole life policies as financial tools?

. . . consider both the qualifications of the insurance representative and the financial strength of the insurance company.

✓ Do they understand the critical design elements necessary to craft a participating whole life policy into a financial tool?

✓ Do they exhibit ease and knowledge in discussing the various aspects of your financial situation with you?

✓ Can they answer your questions on participating whole life with clarity and to your satisfaction?

✓ Can they discuss this approach with you as a lifetime strategy?

✓ Can the agent structure the policy to meet your particular financial situation and the appropriate protection for you and your family?

… consider the corporate structure and financial strength of the insurance company.

The participating whole life policy is a contract with an insurance company so, in addition to finding a qualified insurance specialist, it is also important to consider the corporate structure and financial strength of the insurance company.

Key elements to consider in evaluating an insurance company:

✓ Is the company corporately structured as a mutual company (whose owners are the policy owners) or a public company (where the company is owned by shareholders)?

✓ What is the financial strength and stability of the insurance company (including such parameters as financial ratings [e.g., A.M. Best, Moody's, Standard and Poor's, etc.] and capitalization ratio)?

✓ What is the history of dividend payments—over how many years has the mutual insurance company continuously paid its dividends?

✓ Does their participating whole life insurance policy have paid-up addition riders that are flexible and able to provide the benefits and optimal performance your situation requires?

Participating whole life is a powerful financial tool if the policy is designed correctly. So take your time to find an insurance representative who is knowledgeable and personally uses this approach.

Make sure you fully understand your policy.

Remember that acquiring a participating whole life policy is a two-part process. You need the policy designed and structured correctly to function optimally as a powerful financial tool. And you need an agent committed to helping and teaching you how to use it over many years.

Make sure you fully understand your policy.

Endnotes

Interest for Tables 7 through 10 was calculated according to the Time Value of Money formula shown below and equation inputs (listed by table).

$$i = \left(\frac{FV}{PV}\right)^{1/n} - 1$$

Equation Parameter	Equation Parameter Definition	Table 7 Input Values	Table 8 Input Values
n	= number of periods	3	3
i	= interest rate	Unknown	unknown
PV[1]	= present value	$ (10,000) (starting balance Line **1**, Table 7)	$ (10,000) (starting balance Line **6**, Table 8)
FV	= future value	$12,594 (ending balance, Line **4**, Table 7)	$11,261 (ending balance, Table 8)

Note

1. The Present Value (PV) is always shown as a negative number.

Equation Parameter	Equation Parameter Definition	Table 9 Input Values	Table 10 Input Values
n	= number of periods	3	3
i	= interest rate	unknown	unknown
PV[1]	= present value	$ (10,000) (starting balance Line **1**, Table 9)	$ (10,000) (starting balance Line **6**, Table 10)
FV	= future value	$12,178 (ending balance, Line **4**, Table 9)	$10,888 (ending balance, Table 10)

Note

1. The Present Value (PV) is always shown as a negative number.

About the Authors

Dwayne Burnell, MBA, works with individuals, families, and business owners in developing and implementing a customized financial strategy.

His approach is to educate his clients and empower them—designing a lifelong strategy which builds wealth while maintaining financial control. Dwayne accomplishes this by reducing the risk of capital loss, employing efficient tax strategies, and decreasing interest and fees paid to others.

Dwayne's focus with respect to retirement planning is to create a financial strategy that will provide flexibility and sustained income. Dwayne wants his clients to enjoy a worry-free retirement.

For clients with children, he integrates college planning with retirement planning. By properly positioning financial resources, college can be paid for without destroying retirement savings.

Dwayne's first book, *A Path to Financial Peace of Mind*, was published in January 2010.

Dwayne received his Master of Business Administration at the University of Tennessee (Knoxville). He completed his Bachelor of

Business Administration at the University of Oklahoma (Norman).

Dwayne speaks at numerous conferences and events. He looks forward to the opportunity to speak to your group.

If you are looking for an insurance or college planning specialist, Dwayne invites you to contact him by telephone at 425-286-7298 or 800-266-2971 (toll free). Dwayne may also be reached via e-mail at DwayneBurnell@FinancialBallGame.com. Dwayne is licensed in over 30 states and welcomes new clients from anywhere in the country.

Suzanne Burnell, MSc, has held leadership roles in both private and non-profit organizations over the past 20 years. She has spearheaded change in numerous organizations, executing innovative and sustainable initiatives. Suzanne is dedicated to collaboration and communication.

Suzanne obtained her Master's degree in Earth Sciences at the University of Waterloo in Ontario, Canada. In addition to her corporate and non-profit leadership roles, Suzanne has managed multi-million dollar water resource projects and environmental clean-up efforts in the United States and Canada. She has also lived and worked in the United Kingdom, Europe, and Malta.

Suzanne's interest is people. She is passionate about effective communication and is committed to education. Her business experience and diverse career path make her keenly aware of the power of lifelong strategic money management and financial education.

Suzanne is also a working artist—painting in both pastels and oils (www.SuzanneBurnell.com). She believes in the importance of charting your own course and not letting the expectations of others define you.

Disclaimer

This publication contains the opinions and ideas of its authors. It is intended to provide helpful and accurate information on the subject matter covered. This publication is not intended as legal, tax, insurance, investment, financial, accounting, or other professional advice or services. If the reader requires such advice or services, a competent professional should be consulted.

Although every precaution has been taken in the preparation of this book, the publisher and authors assume no responsibility for errors or omissions. No warranty is made with respect to the accuracy or completeness of the information contained herein, and both the authors and publisher specifically disclaim any responsibility for any liability, loss, or risk, personal or otherwise, which is incurred as a consequence, directly or indirectly, of the use and application of any of the contents of this book.

The example organizations, products, people, and events depicted herein are fictitious. No association with any real company, organization, product, person, or event is intended or should be inferred. Any resemblance to real persons, living or dead, is purely coincidental.

The authors and publisher are not sponsored by any insurance company. Relevant laws vary from state to state. While this book seeks to provide the most accurate and up-to-date information available, this may change, become outdated, or rendered incorrect by new legislation or official rulings. The strategies outlined in this book may not be suitable for every individual and are not guaranteed or warranted to produce any particular results. Readers should use caution in applying the material contained in this book and should seek competent advice from qualified professionals before making significant changes to their financial portfolios.

Insurance Disclaimer

The illustrations provided in this book are for educational purposes only. They are not intended to represent or guarantee a particular result. They are not intended as legal, tax, insurance, investment, financial, accounting, or other professional advice or services. If the reader requires such advice or services, a competent professional should be consulted.

The illustrations contained within this book do not serve to represent or promote a particular insurance company, agent or policy. Results will differ by state, insurance provider, and agent, due to specific contractual design requirements and relevant state laws.

Dividends are not guaranteed and may be declared annually by the insurance company's board of directors. Figures depending on dividends are based on the non-guaranteed dividend scale and are not guaranteed. Illustrations provided in this book assume that the currently illustrated non-guaranteed elements, including dividends, will continue unchanged for all years shown. This is not likely to occur and the actual results may be more or less favorable than those shown. Future dividends may be higher or lower than those illustrated depending on the company's actual future experience. For a complete illustration, see your insurance professional.

Loans on whole life insurance policy cash values are typically income tax-free while the policy remains in-force, provided that it is not considered a Modified Endowment Contract. The policies, as shown, will not become a Modified Endowment Contract (MEC). The term MEC is designated under federal tax law. If a policy becomes an MEC, surrenders, withdrawals, or policy loans will be taxed less favorably than for a non-MEC.

Case study illustrations show one or more paid-up addition payments after policy year 10 that exceed the basic policy premium. The insured may need to provide evidence of insurability before the insurance company accepts payments in excess of this limit.

The insurance products illustrated within this book may not be available in your state or from your preferred insurance provider. Premiums must be paid if the policy is to remain in-force. A policy as illustrated may not be available to all applicants and premiums may differ based on health qualifications.

Life insurance products are not bank products, are not a deposit, are not insured by the Federal Deposit Insurance Corporation (FDIC), or any other federal entity, have no bank guarantee, and may lose value. Life insurance products are issued and guaranteed by the insurance company that issues the policy. Guarantees are based on the claims paying ability of the company.